PRECIOUS STONES

Explains the uses th
precious stones in a
religion, and the pow
– they are reputed to e

PRECIOUS STONES

Their Occult Power
and
Hidden Significance

By

W.B. CROW, D.Sc., Ph.D.

THE AQUARIAN PRESS
Wellingborough, Northamptonshire

First published 1968
Fourth Impression 1977
This Edition, completely revised
and reset 1980
Third Impression 1985

ISBN 0 85030 206 4 (UK)
ISBN 0 87728 458 X (USA)

Printed and bound in Great Britain by
Richard Clay (The Chaucer Press) Ltd.,
Bungay, Suffolk

CONTENTS

CHAPTER ONE

STONES IN ASTROLOGY

The old science of astrology is based on the idea that there is a correspondence between the position of the planets and the signs of the zodiac on the one hand and the events occurring on the earth on the other. Furthermore there is a relation between each planet and each sign with every person and every object on this earth, so that everything earthly has its correspondence with something in the heavens.

Some astrologers, especially in more modern times think of an influence coming down from the heavenly bodies, in the form of some sort of radiation. This, however, is unnecessary. It is suffícent to believe that there is some sort of correspondences, so that what happens to a particular planet or sign will correspond with some event concerning some particular person or thing ruled by that planet or sign.

It would thus appear a simple matter to make a list of rulerships of particuar things, and say that when, for example, a planet has a good aspect, it will be lucky for a particular object, which corresponds with that planet. Indeed some astrologers do tell us that, for certain people, born at a certain time, a particular stone will be lucky, or that on a particular day it will be advisable for everyone to wear a particular stone.

Scales of Correspondence

Unfortunately the matter is not so simple as all this. Granted that planets and signs correspond with precious stones, we will find that different books

give different rulerships for the same. This is not
wholly due to the fact that some writers give the
correct rulerships and others are incorrect, but it is
partly because there are different *scales of
correspondence*, and under one circumstance one scale
should be applied, whilst under another, a different
scale holds good. As the present writer has said
elsewhere, "no natural object is pure Sun, pure
Moon or pure Saturn".

Under ordinary circumstances of course there are
nevertheless certain gems under certain planets,
just as there are certain plants, certain animals and
certain types of human beings. These will now be
dealt with.

In ancient and mediaeval astrology seven planets
were referred to. These included the sun and moon,
which however were also termed luminaries. The
other five are what we regard as the most important
planets today, excluding the earth, for of course the
Ptolemaic system was used (and still is in astrology)
being geocentric, or earth-centred.

In India there were nine planets, for they
included two shadow-planets, the Dragon's Head
and the Dragon's Tail, being situated at the moon's
nodes and thus responsible for eclipses. In native
Hindu astrology they are used to this day, and they
were imported into mediaeval European astrology
and used therein.

Besides the sun and moon the five important
planets, known to the ancients were, in order of
rapidity of movement, Mercury, Venus, Mars,
Jupiter and Saturn. In modern times three have
been discovered, Uranus, Neptune and Pluto, and
these have been used by modern astrologers.

Since 1800, also, a host of tiny planetoids have
become known, but these are scarcely recognized
by any astrologers.

King of the Planets

The Sun is the king of the planets. Because of his brightness, suggested by the gleam of gold, the latter is regarded as the solar metal. No precious stone reproduces this exactly, but Oriental or King Topaz shows a fine golden glow when properly illuminated and is undoubtedly the best representative of the sun among gems. It consists mainly of alumina.

Another kind called Brazilian Topaz is also a very fine stone and consists of magnesium fluorosilicate. It is unusual in containing the element fluorine. It has sometimes been mistaken for yellow diamond. Heliodor derives its name from the Sun (*Helios*, Greek) and is a golden beryl, and is a complex silicate of beryllium and aluminium.

Chrysoberyl is so called from its golden appearance (*Chryse*, Greek) and is composed of beryllium aluminate. Chrysoprase, a form of silica, Chrysocolla, a hydrated silicate of copper and Chrysolite a silicate of magnesium and iron have also been named for their more or less golden appearance. Amber also has a colour suggestive of sunlight, but it is not a mineral but a fossilized gum.

The Moon's Chief Stone

The Moon rules the metal silver and this conforms to her colour. Her chief stone is the pearl, originating from living species of oyster. Mother-of-pearl is found inside the shells of the same. Because of her relation to the tides, the Moon rules aquatic creatures.

Of mineral substances, moonstone or selenite receives its name from the moon (*Selene*, Greek). This stone was alleged to change with the moon. Moonstone is a silicate of aluminium and potassium. The name selenite is also given to a crystalline sulphate of calcium.

Mercury rules the metal quicksilver, first called mercury by the alchemists. This liquid metal boils at high temperature to form a violet vapour. Consequently we feel confident in saying the planet Mercury rules amethyst.

Ordinary amethyst consists of silica, Oriental Amethyst is alumina. Other similar stones are violane, a silicate of aluminium and lithium. Mercury also rules tortoise-shell, since according to legend the classic deity of that name made a musical instrument from the shell of a tortoise.

Stones of Venus

Venus rules the metal copper, since mirrors were originally made of that metal, and the looking-glass is the wellknown symbol of that deity. The stones of Venus are mostly green and it is a remarkable fact that the salts of copper are green, so copper left to rust shows that colour.

The Oriental Emerald, which is alumina, is one of the finest. The Ordinary Emerald or Green Beryl, a silicate of beryllium and aluminium is also one of the finest stones. Malachite, a green carbonate of copper is no doubt a stone of Venus.

Among stones of organic origin, coral is assigned to Venus, for the substance is obtained from the sea and in mythology the goddess Venus was formed from sea-foam. Furthermore the colour of precious coral is often pink, and many corals are cream or white, which is more appropriate to the goddess of love than the blood-red of the war-god.

The latter is Mars, and his planet is called the red planet from its predominant hue. His metal is iron, which often shows a reddish rust. So too his gems are red. They include Oriental Ruby, which is composed of alumina, the scarlet Spinel Ruby of magnesium aluminate, and the Garnet with several varieties which are silicates. A carbuncle is simply a garnet cut *en cabochon*, i.e. rounded instead of having the usual flat sides.

Jupiter, the Sky-god

The planet Jupiter is the largest of the true planets and, next to Venus, the most easily visible. The disc of the planet, in part, is coloured blue. Jupiter is the sky-god and hence his colour is azure or light blue. His metal is tin. His chief stone is the sapphire, signifying wisdom, symbolic of this planetary deity. Oriental Sapphire is an alumina. There is also a Brazilian Sapphire or blue tourmaline, a silicate of boron and aluminium with some admixture.

Turquoise is an opaque stone, belonging here. It is hydrated phosphate of aluminium and copper. There is also bone-turquoise or odontolite, which is fossil bone or tooth, coloured with phosphate of iron. Ivory, according to some, should be ruled by Jupiter.

Typical Saturnine Stones

Saturn rules the heavy metal lead, and his stones are mostly dark. This is in harmony with the fact that he is the slowest moving of the seven planets. Jet, mainly carbon, which is of course black; Obsidian of two kinds, granitic and siliceous, which is generally black Onyx, a form of silica with extremely minute crystals and often marked with white or coloured bands, are typical Saturnine stones.

Jet is of vegetable origin, in fact it is one form of coal or lignite. Later we shall see that the mediaeval heralds included the brilliant diamond under stones

of Saturn. They anticipated modern science, for
diamond is only one form of carbon; the other
varieties (graphite and charchoal) are black.

Uranus, Neptune and Pluto

We are not aware that any decision has been made
by astrologers as to what stones are ruled by the
planets Uranus, Neptune and Pluto. Elsewhere we
have ventured to suggest fire-opal for Uranus, jade
for Neptune and jasper for Pluto.

Opal is a hydrated silica, fire-opal suggests the
magic ascribed to the planet Uranus. Jade consists
of two different silicates and their colours often
remind us of the sea, of which Neptune was the
ruler.

Jasper is a red silica, suggesting the flames of the
infernal regions, ruled by Pluto.

We must now consider the stones to be assigned
to the twelve signs of the Zodiac. A trace of such
assignments is seen in the modern superstition of
birth stones for the twelve months of the year.
Needless to say this silly fad is a complete
perversion of tradition as the Sun does not enter a
sign on the first of each month but somewhere
about the twenty-first. Moreover it is only the Sun
that moves through the Zodiac in one year, so that
when the Sun is in one sign any other planet may be
in any other sign.

Traditional Zodiacal Rulerships

There are three ways in which we might obtain the
traditional zodiacal rulerships, one from the Old
Testatment, one from the New, and one from
Classical Mythology. Unfortunately in all three the
translation is uncertain.

In the Old Testament the twelve stones in the
breastplate of the High Priest represent the twelve

sons of Jacob and their twelve tribes.[1]

In the New Testament the twelve stones of the Mystical City represented the twelve Apostles, each of whom came from one of the twelve tribes.

In Pagan Mythology there were twelve chief gods (*consentes*) each with one zodiacal sign and the stones corresponding with the same were given by Cornelius Agrippa.[2]

The stones worn by the High Priest were as follows, according to the Septuagint: (i) sardius, (ii) topaz, (iii) emerald, (v) sardonyx, (vi) sardius (vii) chrysolite, (viii) agate, (ix) amethyst, (x) chrysolite, (xi) beryl, (xii) onyx. According to recent ideas[3] (v) was lapis lazuli, (vi) probably carnelian, (xi) peridot.

The stones of Mystical City of the Apocalypse of St John were: (i) jasper, (ii) sapphire, (iii) chalcedony, (iv) emerald, (v) sardonyx, (vi) sardins, (vii) chrysolite, (viii) beryl, (ix) topaz, (x) chrysoprase, (xi) jacinth, (xii) amethyst.

In both these sets we cannot be sure of the zodiacal correspondences since we are not only uncertain of the identity of some of the gems, but we do not know where the series begins. The Zodiac is said conventionally to begin at Aries but there is no proof that this is true of the two lists.

Fortunately in the list from Classical Mythology the stones correspond with the gods, and each of the latter was assigned to a zodiacal sign.[4] So we can tabulate, as follows:

[1] *Ex.* xxviii, 17-20. There is a similar list of stones for the King of Tyre, *Ez.* xxviii, 13 in The Septuagint; this is identical with that of the High Priest.

[2] In his *Occult Philosophy*, 1531.

[3] N. Seidler: *Gems and Jewellery*, Odyssey Libary, 1964.

[4] Each sign was the *domus* (house) of a particular planet, the *exaltatio* (exaltation) of another planet and the *sedes* of one of the twelve gods. It is the last names that are given here, although the houses and exaltations will be better known to modern astrologers.

Sign	Deity	Stone
Aries, the Ram	Minerva	Sard
Taurus, the Bull	Venus	Carnelian
Gemini, the Twins	Apollo	Topaz
Cancer, the Crab	Mercury	Chalcedony
Leo, the Lion	Jupiter	Jasper
Virgo, the Virgin	Ceres	Emerald
Libra, the Balance	Vulcan	Beryl
Scorpio, the Scorpion	Mars	Amethyst
Sagittarius, the Archer	Diana	Hyacinth
Capricorn, the Goat	Vesta	Chrysoprase
Aquarius, the Water-pourer	Juno	Rock Crystal
Pisces, the Fishes	Neptune	Sapphire

Now it is highly desirable that the Signs of the Zodiac should have their occult power concentrated in stones distinct from those embodying the influence of the planets. Although each sign is ruled by a planet, the influence of the planet and the sign is by no means identical. Moreover the gods in this list do not always correspond with the planets, e.g. the planet Mercury rules Gemini and Virgo, but the god Mercury is assigned to Cancer.

Forms of Silica

On examining this list we find that sard, carnelian, chalcedony, jasper, amethyst, chrysoprase and rock-crystal are forms of silica.

Sard is usually dark brownish red, carnelian flesh colour, chaldedony pale blue or slate, jasper orange, amethyst violet, chrysoprase apple-green, hyacinth fiery and rock-crystal colourless. These are all in agreement with the astrological nature of the signs except amethyst and chrysoprase.

For Scorpio one would have expected a blood-red stone and some amethysts verge towards this. Some tourmalines, which are complex silicates of boron and aluminium, with other admixtures, would—

make a suitable modern substitute. For Capricorn something black is needed, e.g. jet.

Topaz is a silicate of Aluminium and Fluorine. If Oriental Topaz – which is alumina – is kept for the Sun, then ordinary or Brazilian Topaz can serve for Gemini. The frequently orange colour of jasper serves well for Leo.

Emerald for Virgo poses a problem, as it is assigned to Venus, who rules Libra not Virgo. Moreover Emerald is a form of Beryl, a silicate of Beryllium and Aluminium, which rules the next sign. We venture to suggest peridot or olivine, a silicate of iron and magnesium generally olive coloured, as more suitable to Ceres and Virgo. Olives were an important food, and Virgo was the sign ruling foods.

For Libra a pure green stone should be used, but reserving Emerald for the planet Venus. Jade would be an excellent choice, as Libra rules the Far East, where jade has superlative traditional value. Lastly sapphire is unsuitable for Pisces. Aquamarine is far more appropriate, as Neptune and the fishes are connected particularly with water and aquatic affairs, especially marine matters, so the name of the stone betrays its astrological significance.

The list would then read: Aries, sard; Taurus, carnelian; Gemini, Brazilian topaz; Cancer, chalcedony; Leo, jasper; Virgo, olivine or peridot; Libra, jade; Scorpio, red tourmaline; Sagittarius, hyacinth; Capricorn, jet; Aquarius, rock-crystal; Pisces, aquamarine.

CHAPTER TWO

STONES IN HEALING

Precious stones in ancient days were not only worn for ornamentation. They were worn for their religious symbolism, as shown, for example, in the breastplate of the High Priest. They were also worn for the maintenance of health and the cure of disease. For external treatment they were applied to various parts of the body.

For internal treatment they were sometimes administered by the mouth, but the reader should be warned that in powdered form some are believed to be poisonous, and they should not be taken internally, except under the supervision of a qualified homoeopathic physician. Their poisonous effect is said to be due to the irritant action of the broken particles, which are similar to broken glass! Different opinions, it is true, are held on this matter, but obviously no sane person will wish to experiment thereon.

If internal treatment be desired, we suggest a safer method is to drink water in which the stone has been dipped, or to drink water from a vessel made of the stone.

Mediaeval Ecclesiastic Authors

Most of the ideas about healing by means of gems come from mediaeval ecclesiastic authors, such as Marbodius (1037-1125) and St Albertus Magnus (1193-1280). Such authors lived tranquil lives. The two mentioned, in spite of the fact that both were bishops, lived long in retired circumstances and spent much of their lives in the study of nature.

Many monks and nuns contributed to this subject. We can only give a few examples of their beliefs. Their remarks about healing are often mingled with other matters, and the diseases which are to be treated are not always easy to identify. It is noteworthy, however, that they often appear to be psychological states or psychosomatic conditions, which are well known to be influenced by the imagination.

Inasmuch as the finer precious stones are capable of producing a sort of hypnotic condition of the mind, it can be realized that their healing powers may be, paradoxically, at the same time imaginary (as effected through the imagination) and also real (in producing results).

Beliefs about Healing Stones

We will first mention some beliefs about the healing powers of our well-known precious stones. But, high as some were valued in healing in ancient and mediaeval times, people were more impressed by something new or extraordinary.

For example, the diamond was not much esteemed for healing. Some said it was poisonous, but it had the power of removing poison if dipped in a poisonous drink. Or so it was thought. But we hear more of a still more effective way of neutralizing poison, namely by means of the fabled horn of the unicorn, which was just as difficult to acquire, if not more so, than the diamond.

A whole range of stones, mostly obtained from animals, which will be described later,[1] were supposed to be discovered, and for which the most miraculous properties were ascribed. The situation was not unlike that of today, when a new discovery

[1] See Chapter Fourteen.

or 'breakthrough' in some branch of medicine is announced, and wild ideas persist about it for a while, often followed by a period of complete scepticism.

Marbodius tells us that the agate, according to reports, was first found on the banks of a river, and was named after that river. It not only gives vigour to him who wears it, but endows him with grace, conversation and good manners.

Jasper in Pregnancy

Jasper placed on the body is said to help the woman in preganancy. it was also adopted as an astringent and as a cure for epilepsy. Galen was said to have worn a ring with a jasper, for staunching blood. For most purposes it is worn on the breast. Its power is enhanced if you engrave a kite tearing a serpent on it, still more so if you place it under a stone taken out of the head of a kite.[2]

Jasper protects against phantasms and witchcraft, or so it was believed.[3] Jasper is usually orange in colour but it exists in all sorts of coloured, patterned or marked varieties, the marks sometimes being thought of as significant.

The Varieties of Sapphire

The sapphire, according to mediaeval lore, exists in two varieties. The male shows the blue of the sky, the female the blue of the Mediterranean sea. The former is the stronger for healing, resembling the colour of the firmanent, of which it was said to be a condensation.

The sapphire, according to Marbodius, has very special powers of healing, but only if those who

---

[2] *The Magik of Kiram, King of Persia*, London, 1685, quoted by Fernie, loc. cit.

[3] Fernie, loc. cit.

wear it behave in a very chaste manner. It is
prescribed for profuse sweats, ulcers and eye
troubles.

Epiphanius says sapphire, if powdered, should be
mixed with milk to be smeared over pustules, boils
and ulcerated surfaces. It was also, in powdered
form, dissolved in vinegar. It was applied to the
nose to stop bleeding and to the eyes for all eye-
troubles. It can also be rubbed on tumours. Finally,
wearing sapphire prevents fear.

The emerald, according to Marbodius, can quell
tempests, consequently it can restrain passion. It
favours the functions of the liver, produces bile,
relieves dysentery, promotes childbirth and heals
the bites and stings of venomous creatures.

The ruby, like the sapphire, was supposed to
exist in two kinds, the male and the female, as
mentioned by Pliny. He said the males were more
vigorous and acrid. They protected against plague,
neutralized poison, promoted a cheerful disposition
and banished evil spirits.

The amethyst promoted chastity, was of benefit
to the brain, and prevented intoxication, especially
if engraved with the head of Bacchus, the god of
wine. Its colour often suggests that of wine.

Topaz from Topazion

The topaz is said[4] to derive its name from the island
Topazion in the Red Sea. There are several kinds of
stone, known by this name. The Brazilian Topaz
was chiefly used in medicine. It was regarded as an
antidote to haemorrhages and insanity. It was
sometimes ground into a powder, and mixed with
rose-water, which is probably useless if not, as
already mentioned, dangerous.

[4] Fernie, loc. cit.

Chalcedony was said to cure some forms of lunacy. Hyacinth, says Marbodius, dispels sadness and vain suspicions. Beryl he recommends to get rid of belching or sighing. He does not recommend onyx; worn on a ring or suspended from the neck during sleep, it produces evil and sad dreams. Jet, on the contrary, is recommended by him, for overcoming spells, illusions and enchantments.

Pearls in Acid

We read of pearls being dissolved in acid drinks and being consumed in honour of famous persons. Cleopatra did this in honour of Antony, Clodius (son of the tragedian Æsop) in honour of Cecilia Metella and Sir Thomas Gresham in honour of Queen Elizabeth I.

Unlike most stones, pearl is relatively easily soluble. Pearls, however, in medicine were administered in powdered form, in water sweetened with manna. They were used for consumption and were said to fortify the heart. Among other organic products amber may be mentioned (a cough cure) and red coral (for blood complaints, because of its colour).

Among other stones that have been used for healing the following are among the best known: bitumen, brimstone, carbuncle, chalcedony, chrysolite, chrysoprase, lodestone, malachite, opal, rock crystal and turquoise.

CHAPTER THREE

STONES IN MAGIC

The term *magic* was often used in late mediaeval times for the evocation of evil spirits and the use of their services in carrying out projects beyond the scope of human power. This was attempted very secretly.

However the term may be extended to any attempt to use occult powers for personal ends or even to gain good luck in any enterprise. So regarded, magic includes the use of amulets and talismans. As the use of these was usually to ward off the influence of evil spirits, it is difficult to class this as *black magic*. There is also a mode of divination by precious stones called *lithomancy*.

Summoning of Evil Spirits

The summoning up of evil spirits, even if to carry out good projects, was also invariably condemned by the Church. Furthermore, as it was secret, its methods are difficult to describe.

There are, however, some manuscripts on the subject that have been published, such as *The Sacred Magic of Abramelin the Mage* by Abrahams, a Jewish alchemist and magician, *circa* 1400. From such writings as these there is no doubt that elaborate ceremonies were carried out, coloured vestments and gems were used and various substances burnt as incense.

The theory behind all this was that: there are good and evil spirits of various grades; these spirits correspond to particular elements and planets and particular signs of the zodiac; each spirit may be controlled by the use of salt, water, air and fire, corresponding with elements, and particular colours, metals and gems corresponding with planets and signs of the Zodiac; certain tables of numbers were used; each table was called a *Kamea* and corresponded with a planet and a metal; letters of the Hebrew alphabet correspond with numbers, signs, planets, etc.; each planet has an inscribed symbol corresponding with its spirit, its demon, etc. Thus there is no doubt precious and semi-precious stones played an important part in ceremonial magic.

Although they are not precious stones it may be of some interest to enumerate a few of the substances used as incense or suffumigations. They include, from the vegetable kingdom, aloes, sandalwood, mastic, saffron, myrrh, storax, camphor, frankincense, bdellium Balm of Gilead, Balsam of Peru, Balsam of Tolu, dragon's blood, thornapple and mandrake. The last two were used in witchcraft.

Of animal substances, musk, ambergris and sepia may be mentioned, the last named from animals of the octopus class. Agate was used from the mineral world and onyx and sulphur, both of which are evil.

Amulets and Talismans

An *amulet* is an object, worn, carried or possessed by a person, with the object of protecting from evil influences, and bringing good luck. It is usually an engraved stone or figured medal of metal or some hard substance.

A *talisman* is an inscription, usually on virgin parchment, made under appropriate astrological conditions, with the object of effecting a special event for the benefit of an individual.

The ancient Egyptians had the use of papyri, and sometimes wrote their spells thereon. They also used pottery, shell and all sorts of stones. Some of the most valuable and beautiful are made of the dark blue lapis lazuli. Schist was also commonly used. They were inscribed with animals, such as the scarab and the frog, parts of the body, such as the eye and heart, ritual objects and celestial bodies.

These objects were often buried with the mummified dead and furthermore special figures called *ushabti* were buried with the dead, which are popularly supposed to have been intended to help the deceased work in the hereafter, but the real reason for which is disputed by Egyptologists.

The ancient peoples of Mesopotamia (Sumerians, Akkadians, Babylonians, Assyrians and Chaldeans) often used fired-clay tablets for their amulets. They sometimes cut precious stones, however. Rock crystals, topaz, agate, amethyst, carnelian, jade, jasper and other hard substances were used as seal-cylinders, being engraved to serve both as amulets and seals for their owners.

The Jews had relatively few amulets. It is possible that the *teraphim*, mentioned several times in the Old Testament, but disapproved of by the faithful, were small stone images, as we read of them being carried away from Laban by Rachel his daughter (*Gen.* xxxi, 19).

However, the Jews in later times used certain signs, particularly the pentacle or seal of Solomon, which was a five-pointed star and the shield of David, which was a six-pointed star. These two have often been confused.

The Buddhist Swastika

The swastika was originally a Buddhist symbol, but it reached Europe in the Mykenean age, although not used by the Greeks of the Classical age. It also came to Europe via the Norsemen; hence its adoption by the regime of Hitler in Germany. It is found on amulets or similar objects from Troy.

In China the swastika is often replaced by the *pakwa*, which is probably even more primitive. It is a circle divided into black and white areas by a curved (S-shaped) line. In Japan this was called the *tomoye*. It was also used in Korea.

Gem-stones were abundantly used by the Gnostics, who were a curious group of semi-Christian heretics who were widespread in the first century. They claimed special occult knowledge, which they expressed by very peculiar symbols, carved on stones.

One common figure is the Gnostic god Abraxas, who bore a whip and a shield, and had serpents instead of legs. Uroboros, the snake biting its own tail, is also seen in Gnostic symbology. Abracadabra is probably one of their words.

Arab and Persian Amulets

The Arabs use as amulets the flat bones of sheep and cattle. It is said that parts of the Koran were originally written on the shoulder-blade bones of such.

The Persians, who are also Moslems, although originally Zoroastrians, are very rich in carved amulets on semi-precious stones, especially agate, carnelian and onyx. Both Arabs and Persians use skins.

The making of talismans seldom involved the use of precious or other stones, as parchment was the usual material. Planetary talismans made of the seven metals, with some admixtures, have been described[1] and also talismanic sculptures.

---

[1] A.E. Waite: *The Occult Sciences*, London, 1891.

The shapes of stones vary and on rare occasions show a curious resemblance to the shapes of the objects. The appearance may then be improved, very often, by a certain amount of sculpturing and colouring. Even in *cameos* the cutting out of a figure depends on the selection of suitable materials composed of layers of different colours.

Cameos are usually cut from the shells of molluscs which show this feature. An *intaglio* is the opposite of a cameo. Whereas in the latter the figures were raised on the surface, in an intaglio the figures were cut down into it. Consequently an intaglio could be used as a seal.

CHAPTER FOUR

STONES IN RELIGION

Flint, which is one of the numerous forms of silica (silicon dioxide) was the first material extensively used by man. When we speak of the Stone Ages, we mean those long periods in pre-history when mankind used flints. In the Old Stone Age the flints were unpolished, although often well shaped; in the New Stone Age they were polished and agriculture began. It is certain that the flints were used as tools and weapons, it is highly probable that some were religious symbols.

Old Stone Age carvings suggest a belief in a mother-goddess, who persists – even in classical mythology – as the earth-goddess. We still speak of 'mother-earth'. As flint came out of the earth it symbolized the son of the mother, e.g. Horus the son of Isis in Egyptian myth and many similar figures.

In the New Testament (*Eph.* ii, 20) Christ himself is called the chief corner-stone. The symbolism is of a building in which all the worshippers fit into their proper places. When Jesus called Simon-Bar-Jona by the name Peter, which is only the Latin *petra*, meaning a rock or stone, he was using the same symbolism (*Matt.* xvi, 18).

In the last chapter we noted the close personal association of an individual with his amulet or talisman. In the religion called *fetishism*, which formerly flourished in certain parts of Africa, each individual worshipped a spirit which is embodied in some object, not usually a human or animal figure, but rather a stone or portion of a plant or animal, supplied by a fetish-priest and believed to be all powerful for the individual.

In certain caves of the Old Stone Age certain inscribed stones have been preserved. It is thought that these had the same purpose as the *churingas* of the Australian aborigines. A *churinga* is a flat piece of stone or wood.

When a baby was born, a *churinga* was prepared for him and stored in the sacred cave of the community. At his initiation, which took place about the time of puberty, the individual was brought into contact with his *churinga*. When not in use at ceremonies, it was stored in the cave. After death it was preserved.

Beautiful Jade

Jade is a beautiful stone, taking a high polish. In the New Stone Age it was a rival to flint in the making of implements and had probably acquired a religious significance, as it was used for prayer gongs and sacrificial knives, and also had a medical use for numerous kinds of cure, and a magical use in raising the dead, or so it was believed. These usages were preserved in China and Japan in historical times.

The Maoris of New Zealand used one form of jade (nephrite) for making weapons, tools and ritual objects. In China the jade mostly valued is that known as jadeite to mineralogists. It comes from what the Chinese call the jade country, namely Upper Burma. Jadeite is a silicate of sodium and aluminium, nephrite a silicate of calcium and magnesium. Carved and polished figures of both kinds have been found in Mexico, although it is not native to that region.

The greatest variety of colours in jade is probably seen in China. Green is the predominant – and

usually the favourite – colour. Red, orange, yellow,
blue and violet occur, as well as tints, such as
salmon, cream, apple and mauve. Each of these had
its particular significance in ancient lore.

Although jade is too expensive for building
temples, the very best materials are selected for the
same and sometimes laid out on a symbolic plan. In
the pagodas of China there may sometimes be seen
traces of five compartments each of different
coloured stone, for the five planetary rulers.
Mercury, black; Venus, white; Mars, red; Jupiter,
green; Saturn, yellow. However, there were other
arrangements and the numbers were, by no means,
always five.

In the towers of the ancient Babylonians, called
ziggurats, and in which there are sometimes seven
square chapels, one above the other, each division
had a different colour. But sometimes there were
only five or four, representing the elements.

Jewish Religious Adornments

Jewels, gold, silver, copper[1] and coloured fabrics
played a part in the tabernacle and the temples of
the Jews. We have already referred to the
breastplate or rational of the high priest, with its
twelve precious stones. He also had an ephod, a
tunic, a linen garment, a mitre and a girdle (*Ex.*
xxviii, 4). The lower margin of the tunic had, as it
were, pomegranates, of blue or violet, purple and
scarlet with little golden bells in between (*Ex.*
xxviii, 33, 34). The pomegranates were, apparently,
some sort of rounded precious stone.

Additional to the breastplate were two stones of
onyx, each engraved with the names of six of the

---

[1] Or bronze, but translated *brass*.

twelve tribes. They were put on both sides of the
Ephod (*Ex.* xxviii, 9-12). The high priest also wore
the mysterious *Urim* and *Thummim*, contained in a
pouch. These were probably stones and are thought
to have served as oracles.

It is an interesting tradition among the Jews that
the tablets, on which the ten commandments were
inscribed, were made of sapphire. The holy throne
of majesty (*Ez.* i, 26, and x, i) from which prophetic
ordinances proceeded was also of sapphire.

In the Apocalypse of St John in the New
Testament, two thrones of the Lord are described. In
Apox. iv, 2, 3, he who sat upon one throne was
described as being like a jasper and a sardine stone.
E. Clapton[2] argues that the former should read
diamond, as it is described as brilliant and
transparent. The sardius is a red stone, probably the
ruby. In *Apox.* xx, 11, is the great white throne of
judgement, which is reckoned to be intended for
diamond.

The Holy Grail

Turning now from visions to legend, we come to the
great Christian epic of the Holy Grail. The story
begins with the rebellion of Satan and his associate
fallen angels in their fight against the heavenly host,
led by Michael.

Satan was wearing in his crest an enormous
precious stone, variously said to have been emerald
or a ruby. When Michael struck Satan down, this
gem fell to earth like a meteorite and was found by a
seafaring folk, who fashioned from it a magnificent
chalice. The latter was acquired by King Solomon
and it was handed down to our Lord Jesus, his

[2] *The Precious Stones of the Bible,* London, 1899.

descendant, Who used it at the Last Supper, for the
institution of the Holy Sacrament of His Body and
Blood.

When Jesus was on the cross, the chalice was
used by St Joseph of Arimathea to collect the sacred
blood of the Saviour. After the Resurrection, Joseph
was imprisoned, but was sustained by the Grail,
and he or some of his followers eventually took the
sacred vessel, together with other sacred relics, to
Britain, where it was enshrined for a time at
Glastonbury.

From Glastonbury, the chalice was transported
after a while to a magnificent castle at Monsalvat in
Spain, and removed to the remote realm of Prester
John in the Kingdom of Keriat in North-East Asia.

When the last King of Keriat was killed by
Gengis Khan, the chalice was taken to Antioch and
the last that was heard of it was a rumour of a great
chalice of Antioch which has been looked for in
recent years without success. Claims that it had
reappeared have all proved mistaken however.

The early Christians used a diversity of engraved
gems, many of which have been found in the
catacombs. Clement of Alexandria recommends
them to use, as seals, the designs of the dove, the
fish, the ship, the anchor and the lyre. The good
Shepherd is a favourite picture in the catacombs,
and is also found on gems. The Lamb of God is
another early symbol.

Symbolism and Secret Powers

As persecution decreased, gems became more and
more used to decorate – or even to make – articles.
But always there was a sense of realization of their
symbolism and of their secret powers. Thus the
mediaeval altar was adorned with seven kinds, each
of which had its special place, and that not the most

conspicuous. They symoblized the seven gifts of the
Holy Ghost.

The diamond symbolized fortitude, corresponding with the planet Saturn. If diamond could
not be obtained, rock-crystal might be used in its
place. The sapphire symbolized wisdom and corresponded with the planet Jupiter. The ruby
symbolized devotion or piety and was the
counterpart of the planet Mars.

Topaz represented knowledge and corresponded
with the Sun, because it enlightens. Emerald
symbolized sympathy or understanding, parallel
with the planet Venus. Amethyst corresponded
with good counsel and the planet Mercury.
Chalcedony or Selenite represented fear of the Lord
and had affinity with the Moon.

Christian Religious Adornments

As regards other objects that could be decorated
with precious or semi-precious stones, we may
enumerate the following. The crucifix in the middle
of the altar might be so decorated, but this,
according to the best tradition, should have an ivory
carving of a skull beneath it, to remind worshippers
that the skull of Adam was believed to have been
buried on Mount Golgotha or Calvary, below the
cross of Christ.

The chalice for the wine and the paten for the
wafer are now supposed to be of gold, or silver gilt.
In mediaeval times they were richly decorated with,
or even made of, precious stones.

Each candlestick and the central lamp, holding
the seven lights, ought to have one of the seven
stones aforementioned at its base. The two cruets,
for water and wine, the holy water bottle and stoup,
the font for baptism, the lavabo bowl, the vessels for
the holy oils, should be made of semi-precious

stones, if possible. The thuribles or censers for burning incense should be made of copper or bronze. The sacred picture or icons around the temple should be decorated with precious stones harmonious with their subjects.

Rosaries are, of course, often made of precious stones. The vestments of the priests, particularly the chasuble used for the Mass, require stones appropriate to the colour. The cope is always fastened by means of a morse, which is usually an oblong arrangement of gold, set with numerous large gems. Of the bishop's mitres there are three kinds, used on different occasions and one of these, called the *precious mitre*, is always heavily jewelled. The bishop's crozier may often bear large gems. The bishop's ring bears a large amethyst. A cardinal's carries a sapphire and the pope's an emerald.

CHAPTER FIVE

DIAMOND

Diamond is one of the most valuable, if not the most valuable, of precious stones. It is also the hardest. Its appearance is most impressive, especially in its slightly bluish transparent variety. Its symbolism sets it in a high place in tradition, wherein it has always been associated with kingship and power. Astrologically, as we have seen, it corresponds with Saturn, the outermost of the seven planets. According to Pliny, diamonds have an antipathy to the lodestone.

Indian Source of Diamonds

Diamonds were well known to the ancients. They came from India. Amongst the earliest places to be mentioned in history as their source was the region of Golconda, near Hyderabad.

From 1507 to 1687 Golconda was a separate kingdom ruled by a Moslem sovereign called the Kutb Shah. Diamonds, some of large size, were mined in various places in this kingdom and sent to the city of Golconda for dispatch to the outer world. The mines were ceded to the British but with the discovery of new sources, ceased to function. This region is believed to no longer yield diamonds and is now abandoned, but diamonds are still obtained around Panna in Central India.

In 1728 mines were started in Brazil and in 1868 diamonds were discoved in South Africa, in the region of the Orange River. About sixty per cent of the world's supply now comes from South African mines. Diamonds also occur in the Congo and in

West Africa. Other diamond-yielding localities are Australia, Indonesia, and the Urals in Russia. Curiously enough, diamonds are often associated with gold.

It is well known that diamonds of large size are very rare. It was formerly said that value increases according to the square of the weight,[1] but this is not accurate, as value largely depends on the quality of the stone and large specimens often show imperfections, which have to be cut out.

The Cullinan Diamond

Many fine diamonds are only one or two carats in weight. it is estimated[2] that among ten thousand diamonds hardly one will weigh up to ten carats. The largest known is the Cullinan diamond, which weighted 3,106 carats when discovered and the largest part was cut down to about 530 carats, this part being still, as far as we know, the largest cut specimen.

Diamonds are cut with the aid of diamond dust. But the ancients were ignorant of this art. At first uncut stones were used, then *flat* or *pyramidal* forms were shaped, with little alteration to the natural form of the *stone*, then the *rose* form was developed, with its twenty-four small facets and flat base.

The beautiful *brilliant*, with one end a pointed and the other a truncated cone, was not developed until the reign of George I. Unfortunately stones so cut lose between 30 and 50 per cent of their weight.

Diamond consists of pure carbon. It has a hardness of 10, the highest in Moh's scale, being

[1] The weight of precious stones is measured in carats. The standard or metric *carat* is now defined as 200 milligrams. This is nothing to do with the carat used for gold, which merely measures the proportion of pure gold in an alloy.
[2] L. Dieulafait: *Diamonds and Precious Stones*, Trans. London, 1874.

really much harder than any stone of lower grade.
It belongs to the cubic crystal system and has a
specific gravity of 3.52. It does not show a double-
refraction as many stones do. Its refractive index is
among the highest known (2.41). It is not fusible, but
burns at a very high temperature in air, more easily
in oxygen, giving carbon dioxide. It has the unique
adamantine lustre.[3]

Many diamonds are completely transparent.
Diamonds may be of all colours. Black diamonds
occur, and not all are inferior. Other colours are
blue, green, yellow, rose and brown.

The Koh-i-noor Diamond

Diamonds have played a part in history, as symbols
of royal power and even the prestige of individuals.
Perhaps the best known is the *Koh-i-noor* (*Mountain
of Light*). It is first mentioned as worn by one of the
heroes of the Mahabharata, the great India epic,
which refers to events *circa* 2000 B.C. It is recorded
as passing into the possession of Vikramaditya,
Rajah of Ujayin in 56 B.C.

From this ruler, the diamond passed to the rajahs
of Malwa, then to the Sultans of Delhi, when the
former were conquered by the latter. It therefore
came into the possession of the sixth Great Mogul
Aurungzebe (1618-1707) who became Emperor of
Hindustan[4] in 1658. Nadir Shah (1688-1747), King
of Persia, sacked Delhi in 1739 and carried off the
Koh-i-noor and the Peacock Throne.

After the death of Nadir, the diamond was
yielded up by one of his sons to Ahmad Shah (1724-
1773), Amir of Afghanistan. From one of the
successors of the latter the Koh-i-noor was acquired
by Runjit Singh (1780-1839), founder of the Sikh

[3] Adamant was an old name for the diamond.
[4] Hindustan is the Moslem name for India.

Kingdom of the Punjab, and was worn by him and his successors. The British annexed the Punjab in 1849 and it was agreed that the Koh-i-noor should be presented to Queen Victoria.

The Koh-i-noor came from a mine near Golconda and in the uncut state weighed $787\frac{1}{2}$ carats. It was cut under the rule of one of the Indian rulers by Hortensio Borghese, a Venetian lapidary, who is said to have been heavily fined for making a mess of the job. He reduced it to 279 carats.

When the diamond came to England it weighed $186\frac{1}{16}$ carats and had presumably been recut. Even then it showed several flaws. It was finally recut in Britan to $122\frac{3}{4}$ carats, but is now a perfect stone and my readers can probably view it on visiting the Jewel House at the Tower of London.

Other Large Diamonds

There are records of a very large Indian diamond, called the *Great Mogul*, which was cut to a weight of 240 carats by the aforementioned lapidary about 1665, but it seems to have disappeared. The *Nizam* is another Indian stone weighing 340 carats in the rough state.

Another large stone, in the form of a pear weighing 318 carats or more, was found in Borneo. It was regarded by the local population as a national palladium and a healer of all diseases. It was in the possession of the Rajah of Matan, a local potentate, who refused to part with it.

The *Regent* or *Pitt* diamond was a splendid stone from the south of Golconda. It weighed 410 carats in the rough and 137 carats when cut. In 1720 it found its way into the French crown-jewels, was put on show during the French revolution, was pawned by Napoleon I to the Batavian government but finally found a place in the crown of Napoleon III.

The *Sanci* diamond is a cut stone of peculiar oval shape, said to weigh about 33 carats. It was lost in battle by Charles the Duke of Burgundy (1433-1477), has passed through the hands of the Kings of Portugal and France, was twice lost, once being recovered from the stomach of a messenger, who died in defending it, has been in Russian and is now in private possession in England.

Some very large diamonds were in the possession of the Emperor of Brazil, and were also sent from Brazil to adorn the crown of Portugal.

The *Pigott* was a large diamond of $81\frac{1}{2}$ carats brought from the Indies by Lord Pigott. It was sold in 1801 and again later it was purchased by the Pasha of Egypt. Almost of the same size, viz. $78\frac{5}{8}$ carats, was the *Nassak* belonging to the Marquis of Westminster.

The Orlow Diamond

An enormous diamond of Indian origin is the *Orlow* (pronounced *Orloff*). Its weight is 193 carats. it is recorded that this stone – and another of comparable size – were set as eyes in the head of an image in a Hindu temple.

A French soldier is supposed to have persuaded the custodians of the temple to allow him to act as night watchman in the Temple. One stormy night he forced out one of the diamonds from the head of the image, but failed to remove the other. He fled in the darkness and storm to Madras where he sold the gem to an English captain, who sold it to a Jewish merchant, who sold it again to Catherine II, Empress of Russia. it is still preserved by the Soviet State.

Other giant diamonds belonging to the Russians are: (i) the *Shah*, an oblong stone of fine quality, weighing 95 carats, formerly belonging to the rulers of Persia; (ii) the *Moon of the Mountains* of 183 carats, and (iii) the *Polar Star* of 40 carats.

The Emperor of Austria possessed a very large pale yellow diamond. It weighed no less than $139\frac{1}{2}$ carats and was originally in the hands of the aforementioned Charles the Bold. It was lost in battle, found and sold to the Duke of Milan, then to the Holy See. Finally Pope Julius II, who reigned 1503 to 1513, presented it to the Emperor. It was called the *Grand Duke of Tuscany*.

The Hope Diamond

The famous *Hope* diamond is of sapphire – blue colour and extremely brilliant. It weighs $44\frac{1}{8}$ carats. it was brought from India by Ravernier (traveller-jeweller 1605-1689), sold to Louis XIV of France and lost during the French revolution but found again afterwards and purchased by the wealthy banker Thomas Hope. It (or its largest part)[5] has passed to several purchasers and is still in private hands.

Coloured diamonds of large size and great value include the *Agra* of the Moguls, fine rose pink and now in private hands and one of very dark brown, nevertheless said to have been of very fine quality, mentioned by L. Dieulafait.[6]

The Cullinan, already mentioned, was discovered in 1905 in the Transvaal, South Africa, by an overseer of the mines and named after the chairman of the company. It was purchased by the South African government and presented to King Edward VII. His successor, George V, renamed it the *Star of Africa*. Its two main portions are set in the British crown jewels.

---

[5] The original was cut into two large and one small pieces.
[6] Loc. cit.

Before the discovery of the Cullinan, by far the largest South African stone was the *Excelsior*, discovered in 1893. It was of a fine bluish-white tinge and before cutting weighed $969\frac{1}{2}$ carats. The largest portion, after cutting, weighed $364\frac{3}{12}$.

CHAPTER SIX

SAPPHIRE

The typical sapphire is a beautiful blue stone of high value. The finest are of a deep azure blue and very hard, although inferior to the diamond in this respect. There are also colourless, transparent or so-called white sapphires.

As a matter of fact the typical or true sapphire is a form of corundum and the typical ruby, the oriental emerald and the king or oriental topaz, are all forms of corundum and hence chemically alike, except for their colouring matter. It is the latter that affects the appearance and hence the symbolism. The latter developed in sub-tropical countries, under the deep blue sky of the Mediterranean and the Near East. Consequently Sapphire was dedicated to the sky-god. (Indra in India, Zeus in Greece or Jupiter in Rome).

In Buddhism the sapphire was regarded as favouring devotion and spiritual enlightenment. In the Christain Church the sapphire belongs to the episcopal rings of cardinals, but was formerly worn by all bishops. In astrology it was ruled by the planet Jupiter.

Large sapphires are not much more common than diamonds. The largest specimen is probably one recorded as belonging to the King of Ava (Burma) in the earlsy part of the last century. It was uncut and about 950 carats in weight.[1]

---

[1] There are reports of an equally large or slightly larger stone being found in 1930.

Sources of Supply

Burma is rich in precious stones and is particularly famed for its sapphires, although the number of stones mined has fallen off since the Second World War. Possibly the supply is dying down.

Very fine stones were at one time obtained in Kashmir, but here the production has become very reduced. The stones were of very fine quality there. They are still produced in Ceylon, but are said to be inferior, pale and imperfect. Sapphires are also abundant in Siam.

The earliest stones to arrive in Europe came from Arabia and in the last century were still imported from there in quantity. They also came from Persia. In recent years they have been found and imported from Queensland and New South Wales in Australia and Montana in the U.S.A

Chemical Composition

Although true of Oriental sapphire is composed of corundum, which is a form of alumina (aluminium oxide Al_2O_3) yet other stones have been called sapphires. These include indigo sapphire, more correctly termed indicolite, an aberrant form of tourmaline,[2] and so-called water-sapphire which is iolite, a magnesium-aluminium silicate.

True sapphire crystalizes in the hexagonal system or more particularly the trigonal division thereof, as do all other forms of corundum. Its hardness is 9 in Moh's scale. It shows double refraction and dichroism. Certain sapphires generally of a pale colour, exhibit an appearance of a six-rayed star, especially when cut *en cabochon*. The effect is due to included matter, but the appearance

[2] See Chapter Eleven.

is beautiful, and these stones are called asteria-sapphires or star-sapphires and are highly prized. The same phenomenon is also met with in other precious stones.

The specific gravity of sapphire, as of all corundum stones is 4·0, i.e. higher than diamond, and most other gems. The stone is infusible. Its lustre is described as vitreous.

The colour of sapphire, as of other transparent stones, is due to sub-microscopic particles dispersed throughout, more or less evenly. The substance responsible for the blue colour is now known to contain the metal titanium.

Some Notable Sapphires

Among sapphires of large size that have been recorded are the following: the gigantic specimen, already mentioned, held by the King of Ava (Burma); the *wooden spoon seller*, a brown stone so called because it was found by a poor person selling wooden spoons in Bengal, then sold and sent to Europe. Its weight was about 132 carats and it is, or was, to be seen in the Paris Museum of Natural History, at one time being in the possession of a noble Roman family; another stone in the same Museum and of about the same weight;[3] a heart-shaped sapphire in the crown jewels of Britain.

Other large stones are: a sapphire, worn in a ring by Edward the Confessor now in the Imperial Crown; a sapphire once owned by the Stuart dynasty, also in the same crown; a yellow sapphire in the Sword of State; a sapphire in the British coronation ring recorded back to the reign of William IV; a sapphire brought to Europe by Sir Richard Burton; two large sapphires which

[3] Both this, and the brown sapphire are uncut.

belonged to Napoleon, yielded to him from the Church, said to have belonged to Charlemagne.

Some fine stones are in the American Museum of Natural History, they include the *Star of India* (565 carats) and the purple *Midnight Star* (116 carats); the former is the largest known cut specimen of sapphire. A single sapphire, cut to form an image of Buddha, has been in the Mineral Gallery of the British Museum (Natural History) for a long time. A fine stone of 886½ carats was reported from Queensland in 1934.

There are also some large star sapphires, there is a sapphire alleged to change colour like a chameleon and there are carvings and even cameos cut from sapphires showing different depths of colour or different colours in different parts.

CHAPTER SEVEN

RUBY

There is only one species of ruby, formerly called Oriental Ruby, a beautiful crimson or vermilion transparent stone, of the nature of corundum, but coloured with sub-microscopic particles of chromium oxide.

The stones now called spinels and formerly known as spinel ruby or balas ruby, according to colour, were classed with this stone, but are composed of magnesium aluminate, although the colouration is often the same in appearance and chemical nature. They are now classed as spinel and one speaks of 'ruby spinel' rather than 'spinel ruby'.

Most Valuable Stone?

The true ruby has the same hardness as sapphire, owing to its composition. This , combined with its ardent colour and rarity, make it, one of the most valuable stones and at the time of writing probably *the* most valuable. It is obviously suited to symbolize health and strength in the physical world and action and passion in the astral.

Worn as an amulet, ruby is said to change colour with the health of the wearer or the giver. It was said to darken with illness or approaching misfortune. It is probably the *lychnis* of Pliny, who describes the star variety, and says the latter conduces, favour with powers of authorities.

In Burma, from the earliest times, the ruby has been regarded as sacred. It makes for success in

controversies, disputes or war and is thus dedicated
to all war-gods and the red planet Mars.

Physical Properties of Sapphire

Apart from colour, the ruby has the same physical
properties as the sapphire. It is found in the same
parts of the world, except Australia, but is far more
common in Burma than elsewhere. Most of it comes
from the Mogok mines in Upper Burma. Ruby is
also found in Afghanistan.

The finest examples were long ago in the crown
jewels of the Burmese kings. A famous ruby called
Nga Mauk was one of these and when the British
dispossessed King Thebaw (1858-1916, reigned
1878-85) of the throne they claimed this gem, which
however was never delivered. The largest stone to
reach the West was of Burmese origin and weighed
1,184 carats.

Reports in 1961 of a specimen of 3,421 carats
found in the U.S.A. refer to a broken mass, the
largest part of which weighed 750 carats but none of
it was of gem quality.

A Giant Ruby

Sir John Chardin (1643-1713), a French traveller in
Persia and India, trading in gems, mentions a giant
ruby engraved with the name of a sheik,
presumably its owner, which a hundred years ago
was regarded as the largest in the world.

J.B. Tavernier, another French traveller and
jewel merchant in Turkey, Persia, Central Asia and
the East Indies, records an uncut ruby of 175
carats in the possession of the Shah of Persia.

A round ruby, cut *en cabochon*, was bought in 1653
by the King of Visapur. Another described as
Indian, seen by Tavernier and which he tried to

purchase, was oval rounded $1\frac{1}{10}$ in. long and pointed at one end. It is figured with a slight flaw near that end.[1]

Royal Rubies

A ruby was presented by the Tsar, Peter I (1672-1725; reigned 1689-1715) better known as Peter the Great, to King William III of England on visiting this country in 1697. A ruby as large as a pigeon's egg was in the possession of King Gustav III of Sweden (1746-92; reigned 1771-92). In 1777 he visited St Petersburg and presented the stone to Catherine II (1729-96; reigned 1762-96) better known as Catherine the Great.

In an inventory of the French crown jewels in 1791 there were eighty-one true rubies. One ruby in the French crown was carved in the form of a dragon.

The British regalia also include a number of rubies, but one of the largest, thought to be a ruby, is now known as a spinel.

G.F. Herbert Smith, of the British Museum (Natural History) in a well-known work[2] mentions some remarkable rubies, namely a cushion-shaped rich-coloured stone of 37 carats, reduced to $32\frac{5}{16}$ carats on cutting; one described as 'a blunt drop' in form, weighing 47 carats, reduced to $38\frac{9}{16}$ carats;[3] a very large specimen of 400 carats, broken into two parts of 98 and 74 carats each; a fine stone called *Gnaga Boh* (Dragon Lord) which weighed 44 carats before, and 20 carats after, cutting; a smaller stone, but described as beautiful and splendid, $18\frac{1}{2}$

---

[1] L. Dieulafait, trans. loc. cit. This work gives many figures of famous stones.

[2] *Gem stones and their distinctive characteristics*, London, 1912.

[3] The prices given by the author were very high, but as the value of money has changed enormously we nowhere quote them.

carats uncut, 11 after cutting; one weighing 77 carats in the rough state, 1899; another weighing 49 carats, presumably in the rough state, found in 1887; and last but not least, an enormous specimen of 304 carats weight found in 1890.

CHAPTER EIGHT

TOPAZ

Although topaz is not valued so highly as diamond, ruby or sapphire, it is a fine stone and, from the point of view of occult symbolism, which is largely based on appearance and tactile impressions, ranks extremely highly in the hierarchy of precious stones.

The lustre of true topaz, although described as vitreous, is somewhat superior to that of most precious stones. The colour varies, but the name was originally given to golden yellow stones. They were supposed to change colour in the presence of poisons, just as ruby was supposed to change in contact with disease.

Several different stones have been confused under the name of topaz. they are as follows: Oriental or King Topaz, which is of the same chemical nature as Sapphire and Ruby, and is therefore a species of corundum, it is highly valuable and generally of a light yellow colour; Occidental or Brazilian or True Topaz which is a fluorosilicate of magnesium, and is probably what Pliny referred to as *chrysolithus* but which is not the modern chrysolite which is a yellowish olivine; Quartz or Scottish topaz, yellow quartz or citrine, which is inferior to true topaz in specific gravity, hardness and refractive index. It is of little value.

Oriental or King Topaz is the most valuable, but as it has the same physical properties as sapphire and ruby, and as far as its occult symbolism goes it may be substituted by Occidental Topaz, we need say no more about it in this chapter.

Occidental Topaz is therefore the stone used by the ancients as a symbol of the sun. In astrology it was ruled by this luminary.

Properties of True Topaz

To return to more mundane matters, however. True topaz belongs to the orthorhombic crystal system, it is usually transparent, of yellow colour from very pale to almost brown, or colourless very commonly. There are numerous colour varities, which from the occult point of view are disregarded.

The dark yellow colour is said to be due, usually, to the presence of an iron oxide.[1] In some stones the metal vanadium has been detected. Topaz shows a moderate degree of dichroism, is doubly refractive and shows a fairly high refractive index (1·6). Its hardness, although lower than sapphire or ruby, is still high, being 8 in Moh's scale.

Sources of Supply

Although the so-called true or Brazilian topaz comes from a number of other countries, the stones from Brazil are numerous and many are very fine specimens. They have a wide range of colour, but the most typical shade is of brownish-yellow. Some of such stones, or so it is stated, alter their colour to a fine rose-pink on heating.

The colour is alleged to be permanent, and some of such metamorphosed specimens are on sale in jewellery. From Ceylon come stones of, on the average, mostly the lighter yellow colour. Examples of these have also been subjected to heat, and, strange to say, have been reported to lose their colour.

The topaz also comes from Russia. the

---

[1] In Oriental Topaz the colouring matter is almost certainly an iron (ferric) oxide also.

Koksharov collection, which was acquired by the British Museum (Natural History), contained a fine set of examples of topaz from the region of the Urulga river. These are of pale yellow-brown and are stated to lose their colour on prolonged exposure to sunlight, consequently they have been kept under cover.

The topaz is also found in Queensland, Australia, where the predominant hue is a light yellow, but green and even blue stones occur. Topaz is also found in South Africa, some parts of India, Madagascar and also Japan.

In Europe the true topaz seems confined to Saxony in Germany and Ireland, although it does not occur in Great Britain; as the so-called Scotch or Scottish Topaz appears to be quartz.[2]

Among fine specimens of topaz was a cut, finely polished stone from the collection of the Grand Mogul, which was purchased in Goa over a hundred years ago. It weighed $157\frac{1}{4}$ carats.

This is by no means the largest. Among the Portugueuse crown jewels was a specimen known as the Braganza. This was thought to be a diamond, but suspicions were aroused by its large size, for it weighed 1,680 carats. It proved to be a topaz. This was a very fine stone. There are much larger specimens which, however, are impure and unsuitable for jewellery.

Engraved Topaz

Engraved stones are somewhat rare. The following are mentioned by Dieulafait:[3] one in the form of an

---

[2] According to a recent work (J.F. Kirkaldy: *Minerals and Rocks*, 1963) sky-blue Topaz has been obtained from the Cairngorm mountains, Scotland, however. Those from Ireland come from the Mourne Mountains and are pale or colourless. Fernie (loc. cit.) says small crystals have been found in Cornwall, but they were unfit for jewellery.

[3] Loc. cit.

amulet, in the possession of a writer called Caire; it weighed 29 carats and had a devout inscription in Arabic engraved on it, undoubtedly being of Moslem origin; a white topaz engraved by Jacopo da Trezzo with the portraits of Philip II of Spain and his son, Don Carlos; an octagonal topaz engraved with a figure of the god Mercury, which was in the possession of the House of Orleans; an intaglio[4] with a figure representing Victory, in the Generosio collection at Turin, Italy.

[4] An *intaglio* is the reverse of a cameo, the figure is sunk below the surface.

CHAPTER NINE

EMERALD

The emerald was well known and highly esteemed by the ancients. Pliny ranks it after the diamond and the pearl, others thought it superior to all others. A really good green specimen is so beautiful that it is scarcely possible to compare it with any other gem. It was said by gazing at the emerald one improves the eyesight. It was known to the Ancient Egyptians, the Hindus, the Greeks and Romans.

Among the Brahmins of India, who used precious stones to adorn the images of their gods, the emerald was probably the most frequently used. Moslems frequently made amulets from this stone, engraving verses from the Koran thereon.

When the Incas of Peru were conquered by the Spaniards, vast quantities of emeralds, the most frequent stones adorning their temples, were looted and brought to Europe. The same thing happened when the native culture of Mexico fell.

Emeralds were alleged to change colour or turn paler in the presence of deception and treachery, just as ruby changed with ill-health and topaz with poison. Emerald was said to promote love. It was the stone of the planet Venus among the Chaldeans and classical figures of the goddess Venus were often shown with an apple.

One hundred years ago two entirely different precious stones were known as emeralds. One was: a green corundum, the same in chemical composition, but not in colour, as the sapphire and the ruby, this was known as the Oriental Emerald and still occasionally is so called, but a more modern name is 'green sapphire'. Its occult symbolism is however not with the sapphire, but with the true emerald because this depends on colour. The other was the green form of beryl, this is accepted as the true emerald and has equally fine properties.

Properties of Green Beryl

Beryl has the composition of silicate of beryllium and aluminium. As we have already dealt with two stones of the corundum series, we will confine our remarks here to the properties of the green beryl, which is emerald. This is distinguished from other species of beryl by a colouring material containing a certain form of chromium.

Beryl crystallizes in the hexagonal system, its hardness is $7\frac{1}{2}$ in Moh's scale. It is moderately dichroic. it is doubly refractive and its indices of refraction are around 1·6. Its lustre is vitreous, and it is fusible at high temperatures.

Emeralds today are found in Austria and Norway. In U.S.A. they occur in North Carolina. They have long been known from the Ural mountains in Russia and from Colombia in South America.

Emeralds in Building

Emeralds occur in large masses sometimes, but they are not of fine quality. They may have been used, however, in building. This may explain some statements among classical authors. Herodotus, Theophrastus, Appian and Pliny mentioned gigantic masses of stone, which may, of course, not have been true Emerald, but which were believed to be.

Theophrastus, from Ancient Egyptian writings,

referred to an emerald four cubits[1] long and three thick, which was sent to the Pharaoh by the King of Babylon; an obelisk, in a temple of Jupiter (which probably means Ammon in Egypt) of four emeralds, of forty cubits in length, and four cubits thick in part, elsewhere two cubits; an upright column consisting of a single emerald in the temple of Hercules at Tyre, in existence at the time at which he wrote.

Emerald Statues

It may be that statues were made of crude emerald, as emerald objects were sometimes carved out at a later date. Appian mentions a statue of the late Egyptian god Serapis, no less than nine cubits in height, cut from a single emerald.

These wonders were repeated in the Middle Ages in the stories of Prester John and the Holy Grail. But large masses of emerald have been recorded in modern times from the Ural mountains in Russia. However, the largest pieces are somewhat under a cubit in length, therefore in no way approaching those of the ancient stories.

W. and K. Pavitt[2] mention an emerald as large as an ostrich egg, described by de la Viga. It came from Peru, where it was supposed to be the residence of a goddess.

The largest emerald at present known is probably that recorded as being found in the Transvaal, South Africa, in 1956. It apparently weighed about 11,000 carats in the uncut state.

Famous Cut Emeralds

The largest cut stone of fine quality may be that

---

[1] A cubit was about 18 inches.
[2] In their *Book of Talismans, Amulets and Zodiacal Gems,* available from The Aquarian Press, Wellingborough.

reported to be in the possession of the Duke of Devonshire. It was given in the uncut state to the Devonshire family by Dom Pedro II, Emperor of Brazil, and was exhibited at the Great Exhibition of 1851. It was one-sixth of a cubit in length and nearly as broad, and its weight was 1,347 carats. It is not quite a perfect stone, however, as it shows flaws.

The finest specimen of emerald is believed to be one which was in the collection of the last Czar of Russia. It only weighed 30 carats, but was of perfect quality.

Some excellent emeralds are, or were, exhibited in the British Museum (Natural History).[3] One of these, in the Allan-Greg collection, weighed $156\frac{1}{2}$ carats.

Of cut stones which are recorded in history we will mention two. The first is an emerald used by Nero for watching gladiatorial contests. Apparently the emperor was very short-sighted. If that is the explanation, then the emerald must have been a large one and was cut in the form of a concave lens.

The other is an unguent jar, cut from emerald by Dionysio Miseroni in the seventeenth century for the Emperor of Austria.

The famous Crown of the Andes, made in South America 1593-99 in thanksgiving for deliverance from a pestilence, is said to contain 453 emeralds, of which the largest is of 45 carats. It has been exhibited in the U.S.A.

[3] See G.F. Herbert Smith: loc. cit.

CHAPTER TEN

AMETHYST

Although not so very uncommon, Amethyst is, at least in its finer specimens, a very beautiful stone of violet or purple colour. Its most renowned property, alleged by the ancients, was that it prevents drunkenness. Some state that the very name means not drunken, and is taken from the Greek *Ametho*. This was also the name of a nymph, beloved by Bacchus, god of wine, who was rejected by her in favour of Diana, the goddess of chastity.

Consequently there was a strong belief in the ability of amethyst to quell any kind of passion. It was used for making rosaries, and carving into cups. Drinking out of such cups, of course, could be indulged in without fear of inebriety!

The idea which arose from the colour of this stone itself was, in the Middle Ages, extended to make even violet fabrics magical charms for the preservation of sobriety and chastity. But the very reason for connecting amethyst with drink arose, in the first place, because of the resemblance in colour between amethyst and grapes. Pliny in fact mentioned the name being supposed to be connected with wine and admitted a substantial resemblance in colour.

Violet for Mourning

Violet is a colour used in the West for mourning. Possibly this is connected with the fact the amethyst was dedicated to Mercury or Hermes, the Thoth of the Egyptians, who was, both in Greek and Egyptian mythology, supposed to conduct the souls of the dead in the infernal regions.

Amethyst is one of the finest stones – that does not, for optical reasons – show the quality known in the jewel trade as fire, so this is perhaps the reason for its connection with the dead, and possibly also the reason for its quietening influence.

Amethysts change colour on heating, usually becoming paler. They also tend to fade, probably because of exposure to bright light.

Fine Amethysts

As in the case of emerald there are really two kinds of fine amethysts, Oriental Amethyst or Violet Sapphire, which is a form of corundum and possesses, except in colour, the properties we have already described in sapphire and ruby and will not be dealt with here; and Occidental or True Amethyst, which is a form of quartz. This is the normal form of amethyst and the quartz should be clear and of a deep violet colour. The colouring matter is believed to be chiefly manganese oxide.

Amethyst crystallizes, like other forms of quartz, in the hexagonal system. Its specific gravity is rather low, being around 2.65. Its hardness, on Moh's scale, is 7. It shows double refraction and a certain amount of dichroism. Its refractive index is around 1.55, i.e. not very high. It is infusible and shows a vitreous lustre.

Sources of Supply

Amethysts come from many parts of the world. Large supplies at one time came from Brazil, and when this was discovered the world value of the stone was lowered. Prior to this the amethyst was a very expensive stone. there are now a large number of sources and it is not very rare, so it does not compete with diamonds, rubies and emeralds.

However, the quality of the stones varies greatly.
Another source is Uruguay, also in South America,
where the stones are often very richly coloured,
although on an average not of such good quality as
the Brazilian.

Other places from which amethysts are or were
obtained include Mexico and North Carolina,
U.S.A. also Canada, near Lake Superior; in Europe
in Ireland, France, Spain, Germany, Austria; and
in Russia in the Urals; in Africa in South Africa and
Madagascar; in Asia in Ceylon, China and Siberia
(Kamchatka). Ceylon stones and those from the
Urals rival those of Brazil in quality.

Enormous Crystal

Sometimes large masses of amethyst are found, but
only rarely are they suitable for gemstones. M.
Weinstein[1] mentions an enormous crystal
discovered in Brazil, 1928, which he says weighed
206 lb and was 25 in. high, which provided several
stones of good quality. This far outshines an earlier
discovery of one, sent from Brazil to Calcutta and
which weighed 98 lb.

G.F. Herbert Smith[2] of the British Museum
(Natural History) says that in the said museum
were exhibited a good stone from Brazil weighing
334 carats; a Russian stone, hexagonal, weighing
88 carats; another Russian stone 'with circular
table' weighing 73 carats. L. Dieulafait[3] mentions a
cut amethyst, possessed by the Count de Bournon,
which was half violet and half yellow. Other stones
of two colours have been recorded.

[1] *The World of Precious Stones*, London, 1959.
[2] Loc. cit.
[3] Loc. cit.

CHAPTER ELEVEN

ROCK-CRYSTAL AND OTHER TRANSPARENT STONES

Whilst carbon dioxide is a well-known gas, silicon dioxide, which is from the chemical point of view rather analogous, is a hard solid. The latter makes up a large amount of the crust of the earth. It exists in three crystalline forms; quartz, which belongs to the hexagonal system, crystobalite, which is tetragonal or cubic, and tridymite, which belongs to the orthorhombic, although looking pseudo-hexagonal.

We can dismiss the two latter forms and concentrate on quartz. This has a specific gravity of 2·66, a hardness of 7, a refractive index of 1·55, it is doubly refractive and shows distinct dichroism. It has the usual vitreous lustre. it is found in many parts of the world. It exists in the form of many minerals.

Some of these minerals are crystalline, and may be transparent, as we have seen in amethyst. Of these, rock-crystal is the colourless species. This occurs in masses which are even more gigantic than those of amethyst.

Books refer to a giant crystal captured from Italy by the French in 1797 and which measured 3 feet in diameter. It came from the Alps. Another in the Natural History Museum at Paris is, or was, a mass of rock crystal measuring three feet in each direction. This was found in Switzerland.

A speciment of two feet in diameter found at Invercauld in Scotland is mentioned by C. Nelson

Stewart.[1] Before the widespread use of glass, rock-crystal was made into drinking vessels, bowls, seals and even figurines, but was naturally much more expensive.

Crystalline Varieties of Quartz

In this chapter we will refer to the crystalline varieties of quartz only, omitting what are called crypto-crystalline varieties, namely all the form of chalcedony, which – although often almost transparent – will figure in the next chapter. These consist of very small, microscopic crystals, together with some material which is perhaps not crystalline at all. There is also an amorphous[2] variety, namely opal, which is a compound or mixture of silica and water. This also will be dealt with later.

There are a number of forms of quartz that are, or may be, transparent. They include amethyst, already dealt with; water sapphire, which is clear blue, owing to iron and alumina; Bohemian ruby or rose quartz,[3] pale red from iron and manganese; citrine, a fine yellow stone, a substitute for topaz; cairngorm, which is dark red, orange or yellow; smoky quartz which is brown and morion, which is almost black. The discolouration of the last named is said to be due to sodium.

However, none of these, as far as we know, has any special occult significance, although citrine is in colour correspondence with topaz, and may be acceptable in its place on some occasions.

Occult Tradition of Rock-crystal

It was different with the transparent rock-crystal.

---

[1] *Gem Stones of the Seven Rays*, Adyar, Madras, 1939.
[2] Non-crystalline.
[3] Often opaque.

There is a considerable body of occult tradition associated therewith. One old idea was that rock-crystal was a permanent form of ice. Somehow the ice had been transformed in such a manner that it became unable to melt. This at first sight looks just like a mistake due to ignorance. However it might be interpreted as a memory of an aspect of sacred tradition.

It will be remembered that we assigned rock-crystal to Aquarius, the water-pourer, the giver of rain. According to Sir E.A. Wallace Budge,[4] magicians of Australia and Guinea use rock-crystal for producing rain. Perhaps the original significance of this theory of the equivalence of rock-crystal and ice was that they were both occult counterparts.

Diamond Substitute

Aquarius is a sign associated with magic. Some astrologers tell us it is ruled by Uranus, the magician. Rock-crystal was a substitute for diamond in the early days.

Diamonds were ruled by Saturn, as we have seen, and Saturn was the generally accepted ruler of Aquarius. Diamond was a substitute for black materials, like jet, graphite and charcoal, and was superior thereto. In black magic, shining black objects, like a pool of ink and a sphere of burnished coal, were used for crystal-gazing or crystal-lomancy. Spirits could be evoked and would appear on looking at such objects.

The famous Dr Dee and his assistant Kelley used a polished piece of cannel coal. Kelley contacted the spirits whilst Dee recorded their messages. But the

[4] *Amulets and Superstitions*, London, 1930.

favourite material for this kind of divination was a sphere, ellipsoid or ovoid of rock crystal, set in a stand.

It may well be that rock-crystal has a sort of hypnotic effect, some people having reported phosphorescence and others electrical properties. It is one of the substances used in demonstrating Reichenbach's alleged *od, odyle* or *odic* force. Rock-crystal is used in the mysticism of the *Sufis* and particularly in that of Brahminism and Lamaism.

We must now refer to a few stones which somewhat resemble the seven planetary stones and which, according to some students of the occult, may be used as substitutes for the same, in those instances where they show the same colour.

Zircon

Zircon is a mineral belonging to the tetragonal system, found mostly in Siam and Indo-China, also Ceylon, the Urals and Norway and Canada. It is a silicate of zirconium, and some varieties contain amorphous silica and some contain traces of the rare element hafnium or even of uranium and thorium.

Consequently the properties vary somewhat. The specific gravity, for instance, may be anything between 4·0 and 4·7. it is usually about $7\frac{1}{2}$ in hardness. It is singly refractive and the refractive index is about 1.8. It shows distinct dichroism. The lustre of the finer specimens is adamantine, being the only stones to approach the diamond in this respect. The very rare natural[5] colourless stones of good quality are therefore excellent substitutes for the diamond and are preferable to rock-crystal for this purpose.

[5] Colourless stones are produced by heating yellow or brown stones, however; blue is also produced by heating.

Zircon is represented in a number of different colours. Matura diamond is the name given to a colourless specimen from Ceylon. Jargon or jargoon generally refers to the yellow kind, jacinth or hyacinth to the orange, malacon to the brown, whilst zircon in the restricted sense is used for the green variety.

As mentioned by Huysmans[6] the ancients believed that jacinth cures wasting diseases, drives away insomnia; the mediaeval idea was that it protects against lightning, poisons and pestilences; whilst Catholic tradition makes the stone a symbol of humility. Other authors say it assisted women in childbirth.

Beryl

Beryl is another mineral represented by a number of differently coloured stones. They are often fine transparent stones and emerald is one of them. All of them will have the same physical properties and chemical nature already described for the latter.

Colourless beryl is called goshenite; golden beryl is sometimes called heliodor; rose beryl is distinguished as verobyerite, but in the trade is more often called morganite (after J. Pierpont Morgan, the wealthy financier); the well-known pale blue variety is, of course, aquamarine, whilst bluish-green stones are simply called beryl, without any additional description.

The beryl was used with the object of curing complaints of the throat; but according to another view, its special harmony was with the liver. It may be noted that the throat was under Taurus, ruled by Venus, whose colour was green, whereas the liver was directly under Jupiter, whose colour was blue.

[6] J.K. Huysmans: La Bas, trans. London, 1943.

Beryl was esteemed as purveyor of marital harmony, and acts as an antidote to idleness and stupidity. According to Huysmans,[7] beryl fortifies the will and allegorizes Theological Science in Catholic Symbology. In the *Magic of Kiram*[8] the beryl is called *Panzoon*, meaning 'all-life'. Quite fantastic powers are ascribed to it if a crow be engraved thereon, with a crab underneath, for this makes for joy, wealth and conjugal love in the highest degree.

The aquamarine was one of the sacred stones, as we have seen. Pope Julius II is said[9] to have had a specimen, two inches long, in his tiara. This was captured by the French, but later restored to the Holy See by Napoleon. This is by no means the largest. One was found in 1910 in Brazil, weighing about 110·5 kg. and was transparent throughout.[10]

The aquamarine has the curious property of gaining brilliancy in artificial light, whereas the sapphire behaves in just the opposite manner.

Chrysoberyl

Chrysoberyl is not a beryl, it is a beryllium aluminate (whereas, as we have seen, beryl, is beryllium aluminium silicate). It comes from Borneo, Burma, Ceylon, India, Madagascar and U.S.A. It is greenish yellow in colour. A brownish green variety, called alexandrite, comes from Russia. The latter shows green by day, but red by artificial light.

As green and red were the Russian national colours and as it was discovered on the birthday of the heir to the throne, afterwards the Czar

---

[7] Loc. cit.

[8] Quoted by Fernie, loc. cit.

[9] C. Nelson Stewart, loc. cit.

[10] Photograph in G.F. Herbert Smith, *Gem Stones*, London, 1912.

Alexander II, in 1818, the stone was named after him. These stones belong to the orthorhombic system, have a specific gravity of 3·7, a hardness of 3·7, and are doubly refractive with an index of 1·74.

Chrysoberyl was formerly confused with chrysolite. The latter, however, is a member of the olivine family, being composed of orthosilicate of iron and magnesium. These belong to the orthorhombic system, but have a specific gravity of 3·4, a hardness of 6·5, and are doubly refractive with a refractive index of 1·65-1·69.

This group of minerals are found widely in some kinds of igneous rocks and even occur in meteorites. The term olivine in the restricted sense applies to the olive green variety, whereas peridot is the leaf-green gem and chrysolite[11] is the pale-yellowish.

The Spinel Group

The spinel group of minerals are somewhat difficult to define chemically but are all similar in crystalline form and belong to the cubic system. They include magnetite, previously mentioned, a complex iron oxide, but the precious stones which concern us here are composed of oxides of magnesium and aluminium or, in other words, magnesium aluminate.

The specific gravity is 3·6, the hardness 8, the refractive index 1·72 and they are singly refractive. The lustre is, as usual, vitreous and the gem-stones used are often beautiful and transparent. The spinel ruby, now called, more correctly, the ruby spinel, is of a crimson colour and an excellent substitute for the ruby. The balas ruby, so-called, is a rose-red version. The orange spinel is sometimes termed rubicelle, the blue is the sapphire spinel, the purple

[11] The similar coloured chrysoberyl has been miscalled 'Ceylon chrysolite'.

the almandine spinel, the brown, containing iron, the pleonaste or ceylonite.

Finally, the term spinel in the restricted sense is used for the beautiful blue-green variety. All these have significance only as substitutes for more expensive transparent stones of the same colour. Burma, Siam and Ceylon are the chief countries of origin.

The Garnet Group

The garnet group, from the chemical point of view, include several different compounds but they are all double silicates of the metals magnesium, calcium, aluminium, iron, manganese and chromium. They all fall within a common crystalline form in the cubic system. They vary somewhat in their properties, the specific gravity is between 3·6 and 3·8. The hardness is about 7·25, the refractive index 1·75 or more. They are singly refractive and fusible.

Many of the garnets used in jewellery come from Czechoslovakia. Garnet will be best known through its red species, which is properly termed pyrope garnet, less correctly Cape Ruby. This is fiery red and often closely resembles the ruby in appearance.

Grossularite or gooseberry stone is green. Demantoid or Uralian emerald (because mostly from the Urals) is a brighter green and closely resembles emerald in appearance. Melanite, chemically akin, is black. Topazolite is yellow. Hessonite is orange. Almandine (best from Brazil, but also several other places) is purple. Thus the garnet group provides suitable substitutes for several expensive stones.

The Spodumene Group

The spodumene group includes minerals composed of lithium aluminium silicate, which crystallize in the monoclinic system. The specific gravity is 3·2, hardness 7, refractive index 1·66-1·68, being doubly refractive. They come from U.S.A., Canada, Brazil, and Madagascar.

However, these stones are of modern discovery, with no genuine occult tradition behind them. They include the beautiful lilac kunzite, the emerald green hiddenite, whilst spodumene in the narrow sense refers to the light-yellow variety.

The Tourmaline Group

The tourmaline group, although rediscovered as a popular stone in modern times, included what was long known as *schorl* in Germany and was almost certainly the *lyncurium* of the ancients. The chemical composition is fantastically complex. It is a boron aluminium silicate, with magnesium, iron, sodium and fluorine, hydrogen and hydroxyl. It belongs to the trigonal system. It is found in many parts of the world.

Tourmaline has curious electrical properties. It has the unusual feature of appearing in crystals of more than one colour, often being of complimentary colours such as red and green at different parts and sometimes black at one end.

The colour varieties are as follows: red specimens are simply called tourmaline; pink, rubellite; emerald green, Brazilian emerald; blue, Brazilian sapphire; indigo, indicolite; violet, siberite; black, schorl; colourless; achroite; yellow, Ceylon chrysolite; leaf-green, Ceylon peridot.

CHAPTER TWELVE

TRANSLUCENT STONES

We have dealt with several crystalline forms of quartz which are more or less transparent. There are also some forms of the same that are only translucent. In milky quartz a turbidity is caused by a vast number of tiny bubbles. In prase or so-called mother-of-emerald (which is not really related to emerald) we have a quartz of green hue, caused by the presence of innumerable fine fibres or filaments of rutile, the dioxide of titanium.

In quartz cat's eye[1] there are innumerable fibres of asbestos, and in tiger's eye similar fibres of crocidolite. These two stones are examples of chatoyancy previously referred to. A stone cut *en cabachon* shows a shining line, moving with the direction of light. Quartz cat's eye is greenish-brown and tiger's eye brownish-yellow, shot-blue. Aventurine quartz is a variety containing tiny scales of mica or haematite (iron oxide). It is pink or light-brown, spangled with gold. A yellow variety is called sunstone. Another and very beautiful kind is called iris- or rainbow-quartz, the prismatic effect being due to minute cracks in the crystal.

Types of Chalcedony

A second kind of quartz, as we have seen, is the crypto-crystalline kind, called chalcedony. This again is divided up into several types, of which a few are sometimes translucent. These include plain chalcedony, slate or greyish blue; crysoprase,

---

[1] There is a chrysoberyl cat's eye which shows the same effect.

coloured green by oxide of nickel; cornelia or carnelian, flesh-coloured or brownish-red; agate, which is always irregularly striped with parallel bands of various width, usually milky-white, yellow, orange, brown or red.

Other types are: moss agate, which in place of stripes has inclusions described as dendritic, i.e. resembling branched vegetable growths; cacholong, which is white and cloudy and scarcely translucent; heliotrope-green, spotted red, but sufficiently transparent for observing eclipses of the sun, as Pliny records it was used by the ancients, as was used smoked glass; however it had the peculiar property of changing the appearance of the sun to blood-red, hence the name of the stone which means *turning the sun*. All these forms of chalcedony have very roughly the same properties as ordinary crystalline quartz.

Opal

A third section of the quartz group, termed amorphous, differs from the two preceding in being non-crystalline and containing water and probably organic matter. The specific gravity is appreciably less than in crystalline quartz (2.11 to 2.35 as against 2.65), the hardness is also less (5.5 to 6.5 as against 7) but the optical properties are not so markedly different.

Opal is now mostly produced in Australia. Earlier sources include Mexico, Honduras, Ireland, Scotland, Iceland, Saxony, Czechoslovakia, Arabia and Ceylon.

The classification of opals is extremely complex and involves numerous grades. Few opals are without some milky appearance, owing to cloudy inclusions, all show varied colours, mostly caused by cracks in the stone, giving rainbow effects. These are minimal in fire-opal from Mexico, which is the most nearly clear, but with an orange or red-glow.

In so-called black opal there is a grey or blue background, whilst white opal is very milky, but in both the flashing colours may be prominent. The oriental, noble or harlequin opal is the kind that shows the most brilliant flashes of colour. But there are all grades between these different kinds.

The hydrophane is akin to the opal but has a small percentage of alumina, which the opal has not. When dry the hydrophane is white or cream and slightly translucent, or completely opaque. Placed in water it becomes transparent and coloured like opal, giving off bubbles of gas. Taken out and dried it recovers its original appearance. It was, at one time, regarded as a marvel of nature, and called *Oculus Mundi* (eye of the world).

Symbolism of Translucent Quartz

We must not forget occult significance was even ascribed to other translucent forms of quartz. Huysmans[2] tells us that in Catholic symbolism chalcedony signified charity. Among the Pagan Greeks it signified also great physical strength.

Among the ancient Hindus and Buddhists cornelian was the symbol of joy and peace and was used for promoting good cheer and banishing sorrow. The same is reported by Aristotle and Pliny.[3]

The agate, according to Pliny, was used by the Magi of Persia, for averting tempests. The moss-agate was helpful in promoting the growth of crops, an example of the signification of the doctrine of signatures. Some fine cameos have been made from agate.

[2] Loc. cit.
[3] Huysmans, loc. cit.

The idea that opal is unlucky in a modern innovation. Anciently it was supposed to give confidence.

We now come to a mystery which has never been fully explained. We refer to the widespread use in art of jade, and the fact of the great appreciation of this stone in the Far East, particularly in China, where its symbolic status was higher even than gold or diamonds.

The Chinese word *yu* signifies in general precious stone, but in the restricted sense jade. The same applies to the Japanese *giyukyu* or *tama*.[4] Jade is really of several kinds, but only two are important. Jadeite consist mainly of a metasilicate of sodium and aluminium, which is the rarer of the two, and the preferred kind in China, where little occurs naturally, the main stock being derived from Burma. Nephrite consist chiefly of calcium and magnesium silicate, often with iron; this kind is common in New Zealand. Both kinds occur in America.

Jadeite and nephrite are fibrous, may be opaque, occur in great boulders or rounded pebbles, both belong to the monoclinic system, both are doubly refractive, both show an oily or waxy lustre and both are most commonly green in colour, although also in other colours: white, yellow, orange, pink, red, mauve, violet and pale blue, for instance, but it is the deep emerald-green translucent stone that is praised with religious enthusiasm.

Difficult to Carve

Jadeite has a specific gravity of 3.34, hardness 7, and refractive index 1.66-1.68. Nephrite has a specific gravity of 2.95, hardness $6\frac{1}{2}$ and refractive

[4] G.F. Herbert Smith, loc. cit.

index 1.60-1.63. Both are very tough, although not hard. They are difficult to carve, yet both in the Chinese and Japanese area are made into cups and figurines, such also being found among the relics of the Aztecs of Mexico and the Maoris of New Zealand. The last two named, as well as the Palaeolithic lake-dwellers of Switzerland, had jade axe-heads.

Jade remains have also been found in the Amazon valley in Brazil and in ancient Egypt. C. Nelson Stewart[5] thinks the working of jade is a survival of the culture of Atlantis, the great lost continent of the Atlantic Ocean described by Plato.

Nine Qualities of Jade

Jade was the prototype of all gems of the Chinese,[6] uniting in itself the five cardinal virtues: charity, modesty, courage, justice and wisdom. Fernie[7] quotes the seventh-century philosopher Khivan Ghung as showing how each of the nine qualities of jade reflects the best attainments of humanity.

The smoothness suggests benevolence, the polish, knowledge; the firmness, righteousness; the harmlessness, virtuous action; the spotlessness, purity; the imperishable character, endurance; the visibility of any flaw, ingenuousness; the ability of passing from hand to hand without being sullied, morality, and the ability to sound a note on being struck, music.

It need hardly be added that jade was used in healing. Merely wearing it was supposed to cure the stone by sympathy. As ruling the zodiacal sign Libra and in man the kidneys, jade cures all diseases of that organ or so it was believed.

[5] Loc. cit.
[6] G.F. Herbert Smith, loc. cit.
[7] Loc. cit.

Before leaving translucent stones we must mention selenite or moonstone. This is a gem-stone version of gypsum, which is otherwise seen in the minerals alabaster and satin-spar. Chemically it is calcium sulphate combined with water. It belongs to the monoclinic system. Its specific gravity is 2.57, its hardness only about 2, being scratched by a fingernail, it is doubly-refractive with the index 1.53-1.54. It has pearly lustre, however, and in most respects is an excellent substitute for pearl.

CHAPTER THIRTEEN

OPAQUE STONES

The opaque stones from the mineral kingdom which are most famous are all varieties of chalcedony. They are as follows.

Bloodstone is a dark-green stone, spotted with red. It is common in the eastern parts of India, in Bokhara, Tartary and Siberia, Australia, Brazil and the U.S.A. According to Fernie[1] it occurs abundantly in the Island of Rum in the Hebrides.

According to legend, the red spots represent the blood of Christ which flowed when He was wounded by the spear of Longinus the centurion, whilst He was on the Cross. Consequently the stone was expected to have unrivalled power of staunching wounds and curing all kinds of complaints wherein there was loss of blood. Carvings of bloodstone have been found representing Jesus with His wounds formed from the red marks of the material.

Eclipse of the Sun

Bloodstone was said by Pliny to be used as a mirror for viewing an eclipse of the sun. This is connected with the fact that bloodstone is one of the substances called *heliotrope*. Several uses in magic are recorded in relation to this word, which means 'sun-turn'. One is that the reflection of the sun in the stone turns blood-red. Another, recorded by

[1] Loc. cit.

Fernie[2] is that of the herb heliotrope is applied to
the stone, the latter so dazzles the eyes of the
beholder that the bearer or wearer of the stone
becomes invisible!

Chemically the colours of the bloodstone are due
to iron compounds and it is interesting to note that
iron is the element responsible for the red colour of
the blood.

Closely akin to bloodstone, especially in its red
spots, is the stone called silex or jasper. This is
absolutely opaque, even in the thinnest flakes. The
best stones are orange, but many are mixed in
colour, showing chocolate, brown, yellow, green or
grey. According to Aristotle and Pliny, it cures
wasting diseases, and so Huysmans[3] records.

Plasma is a stone similar to bloodstone, except
that the spots are white or cream. It somewhat
resembles chrysoprase, but is opaque rather than
translucent. Sard is also an opaque stone, akin to
carnelian, but darker in colour, being dark red or
chocolate-brown to almost black. Onyx is
chemically similar, with distinct alternating bands
of black and white. Sardonyx consists of bands of
red or chocolate alternating with white.

Venomous Serpents
Sard was sometimes thought to have much the
same properties as bloodstone. Another idea was
that it preserves the wearer from the bites of
venomous serpents. We have already seen that sard
was one of the twelve stones of the breastplate of the
High Priest and of the Mystical City of St John and
may be ascribed to the zodiacal sign Aries.

Onyx, because it shows the opposition of black

---

[2] Loc. cit.
[3] Loc. cit.

and white, was sometimes regarded as the cause of contention among friends. Indians and Persians, however, are said[4] to use it to protect against the Evil Eye.

Sardonyx, according to Huysmans,[5] in Catholic symbolism, represents candour. Fernie[6] quotes *The Magik of Kiram, King of Persia*, 1686, to which we have already referred in speaking of beryl. Here again it was a question of engraving on the stone two figures, but in the case of the sardonyx the upper figure was a quail, but below it was a sea tench. This was part of a ritual for becoming invisible!

'Fool's Gold'

We must now leave the large quartz group and speak of something that glitters but is not gold. We are referring to fool's gold or iron pyrites, a very common mineral of usually brass-like appearance, high specific gravity (about 5), hardness 6 to 6.5, harder than gold but of metallic lustre, which is unusual. It is a disulphide of iron crystallizing in the cubic system.

A pale species of this, crystallizing in the orthorhombic system, has been cut for cheap jewellery, and is known as marcasite. In ancient times mirrors were sometimes made therefrom, these having been recovered from graves in South America.[7]

Marcasite has found favour in cheap jewellery in recent years. This, because of its metallic lustre, has been substituted by polished steel or even white metal.

[4] Sir E.A. Wallis Budge, loc. cit.
[5] Loc. cit.
[6] Loc. cit.
[7] Weinstein, loc. cit.

Favoured Stone of Ancient Egypt

Lapis lazuli, sometimes said to have been the
sapphire of the ancients, was a very much favoured
stone of the ancient Egyptians. Gold inlaid with
lapis lazuli, for instance,[8] was to be seen on the
mask from the mummy of Tutankhamun, and was
used profusely for the regalia of the Pharoahs. It
was made into figures of the gods and their
symbols.

Lapis lazuli was also used by the Babylonians,
the Hindus and the Buddhists. It was imported
from Afghanistan. It is also found in Siberia and in
the New World, in Chile.

Lapis lazuli is a rich uniform indigo colour,
contrasting beautifully with turquoise, against
which it was set by ancient Egyptian lapidaries.
Lapis lazuli consists of calcite (calcium carbonate)
impregnated with no less than three complex
minerals which are aluminium silicates containing
sodium. It is often flecked with golden spots which
are of pyrites in most instances, although gold itself
has been reported. It has a specific gravity of 2.8
and a hardness of 5 in Mohs' scale.

Powerful Occult Symbols

Lapis lazuli, although a very beautiful stone, is no
substitute for sapphire. Both are powerful occult
symbols. Lapis lazuli is practically opaque, or
completely so. It is idiochromatic. It is of an indigo
colour, and powdered provides the natural pigment
ultramarine. It is of earth.

However, sapphire, at its best, is transparent and
pertains to the sky, is allochromatic and symbolizes
heaven. Lapis represents the earth-mother, sapphire
the sky-father.

[8] G. Posener et al.: A Dictionary of Egyptian Civilization, trans. London,
1962.

Lapis was intimately associated with the royal house of the pharaohs of Egypt. It will be remembered that the pharaoh customarily married his eldest sister. Perhaps this is why, in Huysman's *La Bas*, the stone was supposed to have been used for curing the ill effects of an act of incest.

We must now mention two copper compounds. Malachite, which is basic hydrated copper carbonate, is a fine blue stone, streaked with more or less parallel wavy markings, white or pale and dark-green. It crystallizes in the monoclinic system, has a specific gravity of 3.9, a hardness of 3.5 and it comes from Russia, Africa and Australia. It is a symbolic stone for the Moslem religion and is used for the decoration of mosques. Medically it is supposed to cure cholera and every kind of colic.

Sky-blue Turquoise

More precious, and only available in smaller pieces, is turquoise. A good turquoise is sky-blue, but is inclined to fade. It is, nevertheless, a fine stone, but with a different significance from either sapphire or lapis lazuli.

Turquoise comes from Turkey, Persia and Egypt. From the former at least it is supposed to drive its name. It was at one time mined in or near Tibet, as mentioned by Marco Polo. Today much is found in various places in the New World.

Turquoise is a hydrated phosphate of aluminium and copper and it belongs to the triclinic system although, according to some, it is cryptocrystalline or even amorphous. It has a specific gravity of 2.82, a hardness of 6 and a wax-like lustre.

Again from Huysmans[9] we are reminded that the ancients used turquoise to counteract spells and to

[9] Loc cit.

render them less hurtful, whilst the mediaeval idea was that the stone relieved melancholia and was a cure for malaria and heart complaints. Among the Moslems the turquoise was often engraved with inscriptions from the *Koran*. The stone does change colour with moisture and such changes were supposed to denote the wearer's health.

Finally we cannot refrain from mentioning two stones that naturally show the sign of the cross. *Staurolite* is a hydrated aluminium iron silicate, usually opaque, but sometimes more or less transparent, brown in colour. It has a specific gravity of 3.4 to 3.8 and a hardness of 7 to 7.5, but the curious feature lies in the crystals, which belong to the orthorhombic system and which often appear in the form of a Greek cross.[10]

The other stone is chiastolite, an aluminium silicate which contains black inclusions of carbonaceous matter, which may often be seen marked out on the surface in the form of a cross.

[10] A cross with equal arms.

CHAPTER FOURTEEN

STONES OF ORGANIC ORIGIN

Besides the mineral kingdom, both the plant kingdom and the animal kingdom produce some products of great beauty and many of extraordinary curiosity. We will mention a few examples, of which only jet, amber, coral and pearl have any claim to appear as gems.

But first it is worth mentioning those microscopic members of the vegetable kingdom, existing in infinite numbers in the sea and often abundant in fresh water, in which each is provided with two valves of transparent silica as a shell, and each valve is sculptured in a complex regular pattern distinctive of the species.

Had these patterns been visible to the unaided eye, the species might have been used as gems or ornaments. They are, as skeletal remains, deposited in vast numbers at the bottom of the sea, where they form diatomite or kieselgühr, a whitish brown powder when dried, which has several uses.

Some brown and red seaweeds, although a minority, secrete masses of calcareous material resembling coral – they are called corallines or nullipores as having no openings.

Jet

Land plants produce quantities of wood, sufficient for use in most trees. If this gets fossilized we may occasionally find some transformed into wood-opal. Vast quantities of extinct vegetation has been transformed into coal, but under certain circumstances of fossilization, jet is formed from the wood of cone-bearing plants.

Jet has a specific gravity of 1.2 to 1.4 and a hardness on an average of about 3.75. To jet was ascribed healing powers, especially in toothache, migraine, epilepsy and tumours. For the latter it was made into an ointment with beeswax. It was also used in various religions, including the Christian, for amulets, and was supposed to ward off the effects of the evil eye. Rosaries were sometimes made from it.

In the late years of the reign of Queen Victoria in this country, jet was much used for mourning jewellery. Jet was used by the ancients, and even in Bronze Age times. It is now found in Spain, France and Germany and Whitby in Yorkshire was famed for it.

Vegetable ivory is the endosperm (food storage material, a variety of cellulose[1]) of the seeds of the rather peculiar tropical American palms of the genus *Phytelephas*.[2] The fruits of these look somewhat like coconuts and the seeds are correspondingly large. Vegetable ivory has a specific gravity of 1.4 and is thus much lighter than the animal ivories. It also has a finger grain.

Resins

Resins are derived from various plants. They are secretions from them, rather than being actual tissues like woods. Some resins are not only of considerable monetary value, but have extraordinary significance both in magic, medicine and religion.

It will be remembered that three wise men from

---

[1] *Cellulose*, as forming the cell walls of all land plants and many of those of the sea, is one of the most abundant of all substances. Combined with the *lignin* it forms wood. Cellulose however does not usually act as storage material. For that purpose starch is most common.

[2] This name means 'plant-elephant'.

the East visited the infant Jesus and presented Him
with gold, frankincense and myrrh. In sacred
tradition they were magi, in other words, priest-
kings. Their names are usually given as Melchior,
King of Nubia; Balthazar, King of Chaldea and
Gaspar, King of Tarshish or King of Ethiopia.
Melchior presented gold, signifying kingship;
Balthazar offered frankincense, denoting priesthood
and Gaspar offered myrrh, indicating sacrifice, as it
was used in embalming.

Only one resin, and that fossilized, ranks as a
semi-precious stone and that is amber. It is derived
from coniferous trees and mostly occurs in the
Baltic region. It has a specific gravity of 1.08, a
hardness of 2.5 and it is usually of translucent
golden-yellow appearance, although other colours
appear. It was mostly formed in the geological age
called the Oligocene, which lasted for several
millions of years and ended nearly twenty million
years ago.

Amber is of great interest to the biologist. Small
organisms, many of them now extinct, at least in
the northerly region where the amber is found,
occur as inclusions, as they were stuck in the amber
when it was a sticky liquid. They include mostly
insects, centipedes, also spiders, some pseudoscor-
pions, earthworms, small snails and one or two
lizards.[3] As inclusions one also finds leaves, flowers,
small twigs, feathers of birds and hairs of
mammals.[4]

Amber in Medicine
Amber was used for decoration in prehistoric and
ancient times, and among the Greeks and Romans
carvings were in vogue. Pliny complains that a

[3] A Lizard in amber is figured in L. Dieulafait, loc cit.
[4] For details see Willy Ley: *Dragons in Amber*, New York, 1951.

small amber figure costs more than a healthy slave! Amber was used in medicine, even internally, powdered and mixed with honey. It was also used as incense. Even worn, it was said to protect health. It was specially favoured for toothache, headache and rheumatic pains of all kinds. It was applied to wounds to stop bleeding, and worn to reduce goitre.

In magic, amber protects against bad luck and the attacks of witches, owing to its rulership being under the glorious Sun and because of its electrical properties.

Large pieces of amber are rare. Dieulafait[5] mentions one in the Museum at Berlin which weighed 18 lb.

True Corals

Turning now to the animal kingdom, we find numerous species of microscopic Foraminifera, many worms and plant-like animals (Polyzoa) forming extensive deposits of calcareous material, but the true corals are animals more or less related to sea anemonies, sea-pens, sea-fans and jelly-fishes.

Coral, in fact, is skeletal material, forming a core or base to the animals, which cling together in vast collections called colonies. In black corals this material is horny, in the madrepores or stony corals each individual is placed on a white stone-like cup divided by radiating partitions, in the millepore corals there are simple pit-like markings, whilst in the alcyonarian corals we have various shapes and colours, including blue corals, organ-pipe corals and precious corals.

In organ-pipe corals the skeletal mass consists of calcareous tubes side by side, resembling miniature

[5] Loc. cit.

organ pipes, pink in colour. Precious coral appears in branched cylindric masses, usually not more than about half an inch in diameter and varying from deep red to almost white. It comes from the species *Corallium rubrum*.

Corals are found in all warm shallow seas and are abundant in the Mediterranean and off the coasts of Japan. The specific gravity is 2.65, its hardness about 3.75.

Coral has been used from the earliest times in medicine and magic. It has all the usual properties of curing almost everything by external, or internal use, or merely by being worn. It also protects against many evils, including witchcraft, the evil eye and sterility. The wearing of coral by children is a custom remaining from Roman times. Coral is used for rosaries and often made into bead necklaces and bracelets.

Coral consists of calcium carbonate, mixed with a little magnesium carbonate and some organic material. The calcium carbonate is in the form of calcite, which belongs to the hexagonal system.

Molluscs (Shellfish)

The great group of the Mollusca (molluscs) or shellfish, build their shells of calcium carbonate, usually in two layers, one of the aforesaid calcite, the other of aragonite, another crystalline form of the same substance, belonging to the orthorhombic system. The last named is inside the former and often consists of a series of plates forming mother-of-pearl. Outside the shell is a layer of organic substance, conchiolin, and the same is mixed with the calcareous layers.

Shells were used as ornaments and probably for healing and magic by the earliest known prehistoric men. Later the cowrie shell, in the heliolithic culture, acquired a magical reputation and was much sought after.

Pearls

As is well known, pearls are forms within certain molluscs in much the same way as the inner layer of the shell, the mother-of-pearl. The calcareous layers are deposited in a concentric manner around a tiny parasite or irritant particle. The best pearls are therefore spherical or oval. Some are formed attached to the shell. Naturally these are of less value and are called *blister pearls*.

Very large pearls tend to grow in an irregular manner and are called *baroque pearls*. Pearls grow in a variety of bivalve molluscs. Most of those found in jewellery come from the pearl-oyster (*Pinctada*), some from the so-called pearl mussel (*Margaritifera*).

Like coral, pearls are obtained from warmer seas. A few are derived from freshwater species of the *Unio* family. The largest pearl in the world (in private hands in America) is said to be $9\frac{1}{2}$ inches in length and $5\frac{1}{2}$ inches across and to have been taken from the largest species of bivalve mollusc, a giant clam of the genus *Tridacna*.

The jeweller Tavernier, who travelled in the East in search of gems in the seventeenth century, mentions a pearl of the size of a small pear in the possession of the Shah of Persia. Another interesting pearl is the *Great Southern Cross*, fished up off Western Australia in 1886 and resembling nine large pearls fitted together in the form of a Latin Cross.

The largest perfectly spherical pearl may be the one called *La Pellegrina* in a Museum at Moscow in

1912 according to G.F. Herbert Smith.[6] It was white in colour and of Indian origin and weighed 28 carats.[7] Where it is now, if it has survived, we are unaware. Pearls are of various colours, the most valuable being white, then pink or black; yellow or blue are less favoured. Cultured pearls and artificial pearls are outside the scope of our subject.

Religious Associations

Being formed by damage to the shellfish body, as has been known from ancient times, pearls have been thought to signify sorrow. Their rare pearly lustre and colour has suggested purity.

In the *New Testament* the pearl signifies the Gospel itself. In the *Kebra Nagast* or *Book of the Glory of Kings*[8] giving the traditional history of religion in Ethiopia and the patent of Sovereignty of Abyssinia, it is related that salvation descended into the body of Adam in the form of a pearl. This pearl did not go to Cain or Abel but descended unto Seth. From him it passed to Noah, Abraham, Isaac, Jacob, Judah, David and Solomon. And from the latter it was to pass through his son Rehoboam, eventually coming to Joachim and Anna to Mary, thus to Jesus the Saviour.

And the angel Gabriel was directed to protect all who carry the pearl, Michael to direct and keep Zion, the tabernacle wheresoever the pearl goeth and Uriel, it was said, keeps the wood which shall become the Cross of Christ. Thus the pearl was recognized as the pre-existing and eternal Lord Jesus, and was thought of as the chief stone of the

---

[6] Loc. cit.

[7] Pearls are more often weighed in grains; the figure here gives is more suited for comparison.

[8] Translated by Sir E.A. Wallis Budge as *The Queen of Sheba and her only son Menylek*, London, 1932.

Christian religion. Mary would be represented by mother-of-pearl.

The Jewel in the Lotus

It reminds one of the Buddisht prayer: *Om mani padme, Hum* (Hail thou jewel in the lotus, Amen.) The jewel is the Supreme God, the lotus is the womb of the Mother. It is very similar to the *Ave Maria.*

Curiously enough, in the celebration of the Mass the term *Margarita,* that is Pearl, is used for the Consecrated Particle dropped into the Chalice, whereby the Body of Christ is united with His Sacred Blood. And in the Eastern Rite it is applied to each Particle placed in the chalice and administered to the faithful by means of a spoon.

The group of animals called the Mollusca includes the squid, the cuttlefish and the octopus, all classed in the subdivision *Cephalopoda* because they have their appendages around the head. This group includes the dreaded kraken or devil-fish. They emit the substance sepia, and some of them provide so-called cuttle-bone.

Leaving the Mollusca, we come to the great group of the Arthropoda, the jointed-legged animals. They are subdivided into a number of groups, such as the crustaceans, insects and the spider-scorpion class. The crustaceans include crayfish, lobsters, crabs, shrimps and prawns. Many of them yield a stone called *the crab's eye,* which is not an eye at all but a calcareous mass from the gizzard. It was used in healing.

Turning now to Vertebrata, these are the only animals that possess true bone. Many curious ideas have been associated with bone. One of the strangest of all natural curiosities is the skull of a marine cat-fish of South America. This on its lower

surface represents a close resemblance to a crucifix.
Not only is the figure shown on the cross, with a
halo, but appended bones represent the
instruments of the passion; the spear, the dice and
the nails.

The Sacred Bone

In the human body, as in those of other land
vertebrates, there is a portion of the backbone,
between the hip bones, that is called the *sacrum* or
sacred bone. The old Jewish rabbis called it *luz* or
luez. Its sacred character pertains to the fact that it
was believed to be indestructible. It remained when
all the rest of the body had been destroyed, and was
the nucleus of the resurrection body. It is obviously
a symbol of what theosophists called the *causal body*,
which persists from incarnation to incarnation.[9]

Many stones, believed to have strange virtues,
were recorded by mediaeval writers as being found
in the bodies of vertebrate animals. Shakespeare, in
his *As You Like It*, refers to *toad-stone*, found in the
head of that animal. In fact rings, said to contain
that stone, actually exist.

Sir Ray Lankester, the famous zoologist in the
early part of the present century,[10] actually
examined a number of such rings in the British
Museum, London and the Ashmolean Museum,
Oxford and found that the majority were rounded
flattened teeth from the palate of the fossil fish
Lepidotus. They were from ancient rock of
Cretaceous age and were discoloured (drab or even
black) by long ages of fossilization.

---

[9] Some thesophists claims that an actual physical atom or unit of
some sort so persists.

[10] Recorded in his *Science from an Easy Chair*, a second series, 3rd
edition, London, 1912.

The mineral asbestos is sometimes called *salamander's feather*. But salamanders have no feathers. The name arises from the belief that salamanders can live in fire and, as is well known, asbestos is fire resistant.

Turning now to reptiles we find there are references to an *adder-stone*, but on inquiry we find it to be purely imaginary and no doubt the story originates from that of the druidical serpent's egg, already described elsewhere.

Origin of Tortoise-shell

An ornamental substance of some value is produced by reptiles, namely tortoise-shell. This mostly is derived, not from land tortoises, but the marine species called the hawk's bill turtle. It comes from tropical seas. It is formed from the outer skin (epidermis) and consists of keratin, containing microscopic patches of the red pigment carotin. Its specific gravity is round about 1.3.

Horn and hair are also formed from the outer skin and consist of keratin, whereas in antlers the outer skin is soft and peels off, leaving bone. In a cow's horn the inner core is bone. Bone is chemically different from horn and shell and consists largely of calcium phosphate. It has a specific gravity of 2.

Rhinoceros horn consists of fibrous keratin throughout. It has long been believed that cups made from it prevent poisoning, and it has been highly prized, especially in the East. Some species of rhinoceros, it is said, have practically been exterminated in the quest for their horns.

Whalebone is found as plates in the mouth of some whales and is akin to horn.

Ivory

Ivory is the main material of teeth and is, of course, only obtained in quantity from animals like the hippopotamus, walrus, elephant, mammoth and narwhal with enormous tusks. The last named is a member of the whale group in which the males have one projecting tooth which may reach up to nine feet in length (the rest of the animal may attain fifteen feet in length).

It is the narwhal tooth that has been alleged to form the horn of the mythical unicorn. This has a reputation even greater than the horn of the rhinoceros for protecting against poison, for which purpose it was scraped or powdered. The complete tusk was used as a sceptre.

Ivory has a specific gravity of between 2 and 3 and a chemical composition resembling very compact bone. Immense tusks come from the fossil mammoth.

Fossil ivory, from the extinct mammoths and mastodons, sometimes gets impregnated with iron phosphate which imparts a blue colour. It is then called odontolite. Similarly bone forms what is called bone turquoise. The blue tends to fade in the light.

Pathological Concretions

Many birds and mammals, like the human subject, tend to develop stones, which are pathological concretions or calculi.[11] They are found in all parts of the body, especially in ducts and hollow organs.

The present-writer has handled a stone, nearly as big as a football, removed by a veterinary friend from a horse. The most famous stone of this kind is the *bezoar*, very common in goats and stags. It was

[11] *Sing.* Calculus.

thought to protect against poisons and often had an agreeable smell. It was mounted in silver and gold and the smaller ones were worn on rings. Pope Innocent XI (r. 1676-89) collected a large number of such rings whilst he was a cardinal.

Similar stones have been reported from the hyaena and from various birds, namely the swallow, hoopoe, cock, eagle and the mythical phoenix. Among the birds the stones were sometimes said to have been found in the nest, which is quite possible, as they are sometimes regurgitated.

We will conclude by reference to a very valuable substance, namely ambergris. It is a substance of low specific gravity around 0.8 or 0.9, therefore floating, light grey in colour and with a powerful odour. It is thrown up from the intestines of the sperm whale (*Physeter macrocephalus*). It has a remarkable power of bringing out other odours, when mixed with various scents. Hence it is highly prized in the perfumery industry.

INDEX